THE AUTHOR

Bernard S. Morris is Professor of Government at
Indiana University, where he teaches courses in political theory, Soviet foreign policy, and communism.
He has also taught at The American University and
has served as an Intelligence Specialist in the Department of State. He has written extensively on
communist affairs in professional journals, and is a
contributor to *Politics in the Soviet Union: 7 Cases*,
and *The Communist States and the West*.

International
Communism and
American Policy

BERNARD S. MORRIS

INDIANA UNIVERSITY

International Communism and American Policy

ATHERTON PRESS · NEW YORK
1966

To BETTY, TONY, *and* SAMMY, *who cheerfully followed me into the wilderness*

PREFACE

This volume represents an attempt to place in perspective the schism in the international communist movement and in some measure to relate American policy to this historic world event. Justification for yet another book on communism rests on the impression that while the Sino-Soviet dispute has been expertly chronicled and analyzed, relatively little has been written to place the schism in historical and institutional perspective or to examine the United States position in critical terms. Part I presents a schema of the changes that have occurred in the structure of authority and control of the communist movement over the decades and, hopefully, suggests some of the factors affecting both its unity and its polycentric drift. Part II deals with the American reception of the split in international communism and of Khrushchev's policy of accommodation with the United States, which figured as a major factor in the Soviet-Chinese split.

Whatever advantages this essay form affords the author in presenting his ideas in relatively brief compass, it admittedly suffers in failing to do justice to the complexities of the subject matter. In focusing, for example, on the psychopolitical reasons behind the cohesion of the international movement rather than on the overworked aspect of Moscow's domination of it—that is, on a rigid control model in which virtual omnipotence is attributed to the ruling élite—I have neglected a precise analysis of the changing motives of those who have moved into and out of the communist parties for more than four decades and of the very consequences of organizational manipulation and machine politics on the international structure. Similarly, I have tried to demonstrate that the development of international communism has been conditioned by American attitudes and foreign policy, but I have not, for example, detailed American political intervention in the affairs of certain countries—many of them friendly—to subvert the communist parties. Much of the crucial evidence needed to do justice to this aspect of American/communist affairs is unavailable. In the same way, the unavailability of the Comintern archives prevents a definitive portrayal of the stresses and strains in international communism. The role of authority in the international communist movement as well as the interrelationship of American policy and communism remain fertile fields for the investigator. If I have merely made some suggestive comment on these topics which is intelligible for the most part to the general reader as well as the specialist, I shall be satisfied.

ACKNOWLEDGMENTS

It is my poignant duty to acknowledge my debt to Otto Kirchheimer who read the entire manuscript just before his death. The world has lost a fine scholar and I, a dear friend.

I am also indebted to Morris Watnick who criticized the first part of the manuscript; to Herbert Marcuse and Samuel L. Sharp without the benefit of whose friendship I would be far more ignorant about man and politics; and to my former colleagues in the Department of State, anonymous by tradition, from whose association I profited.

May I also express my appreciation to the librarians of the Hoover Institution and the Department of State for their courtesies; to the Ford Foundation for making two teaching-free summers available; and to Edward H. Buehrig for his quiet encouragement.

Finally, I am especially indebted to Mrs. Helen E. Buchholz, old friend and former colleague, for preparing the Index.

Though I hope that the afore-mentioned—and others —subscribe to all or some of my views, I alone am responsible for what is written.

CONTENTS

PART I

Authority and Control in the
International Communist
Movement

1. THE STRUCTURE OF AUTHORITY

In the public mind, international communism has been viewed as a cohesive, disciplined movement bound by a common ideology subject to the dictates of Moscow. The national communist parties and their subsidiary organizations were subordinated to the policy preferences of Moscow. In no major policy shift did the parties deviate from the requirements laid down by the Moscow center. Communist leaders and cadres were distinguished by their subservience and obsequiousness. Monolithic unity was the hallmark of international communism, a view proclaimed by the Communists themselves and accepted by the non-communist public at large. The behavior of the communist movement under Stalin's rule gave ample support to this conception.

Paradoxically, however, the history of the communist movement may be written as a record of deviation and dissension. The Trotskyist opposition of the 1920s and 1930s, the Titoist defection of the 1940s, the Chinese schism in the late 1950s, and the defection in the 1960s of a number of communist parties and communist party factions from the Soviet orbit are the highlights of the centrifugal tendency in international communism. A significant but less dramatic aspect of this tendency is the record of individuals who have resigned, defected, and been expelled from the parties as a result of disaffection for policy or other reasons. The loss of membership after the conclusion of the Nazi-Soviet Pact was one of the more obvious cases of a pattern of turnover that has been endemic to the communist movement. In a sense, the vaunted unity of the movement was secured by constantly replacing the disaffected with candidates whose memories were shorter or for whom previous policy shifts were irrelevant.[1] What effect this turnover of membership had on a particular party's potential for growth and influence is another—and speculative—question. The unity of the parties, therefore, does not presuppose the idea of a long-term and committed membership; indeed it may be argued that the unity of the parties was secured in spite of the fickleness of the rank and file. Unity represents rather the allegiance of the national parties to Moscow, more specifically the allegiance of the party leaderships. For the record is clear: until 1953, with the notable exception of Tito, Stalin was able to command the allegiance of the national leaderships, including the Chinese Communists, through all manner of policy shifts. Where the leadership posed a problem—or might have posed a problem—Stalin was able to secure substitutes.

Following Stalin's death, however, the pattern of automatic subordination of the national communist leaderships to Moscow was shattered. Unity gave way to polycentrism—that is, to the assertion of independence or autonomy in a variety of spheres by certain national leaderships. This fragmentation of the communist movement is in essence the consequence of the breakdown of authority heretofore wielded by the Soviet Communists.[2] The Soviet party is no longer able to rely upon the undeviating loyalty of all communist parties. Not only China but little Albania, not only the New Zealand Communist Party, far removed from the USSR geographically, but even the Rumanian party, located within its immediate sphere of influence, has defied Soviet leadership. Explanation of this development is no doubt complex, but the central issue is the role of authority. This inquiry, therefore, begins with the concept of authority as it developed in the international movement from its origins.

On the face of it, an inquiry into the sources of authority in the international communist movement would appear to be a belaboring of the obvious. For most of the movement's history, was not all authority lodged in the person of J. V. Stalin? Did he not command only to be obeyed? Was not his interpretation of communist ideology the only correct interpretation? To be sure, but the description of communist performance does not explain how he was able to act in this command role and even less why anyone obeyed him. For authority implies a two-way relationship between ruler and ruled, in which a certain measure of freedom is available to the latter, except perhaps in circumstances of direct physical domination. By and large, Stalin did not have at his disposal in a foreign country the machinery of violence that was available to him in the Soviet Union and could be used to eliminate a recalcitrant party member. The relationship between Stalin and a party leader in an area outside his physical control was not based merely on force or on the threat of force; a subtler relationship formed the basis of the structure of authority.[3] Reversing the argument, if Stalin were the sum and substance of authority, the communist movement should automatically have fallen apart when he died in 1953. Although the removal of the authoritative figure from the scene certainly did complicate Soviet internal politics, it did not in the first instance affect the allegiance of the communist parties to Moscow, precisely because their loyalty was extended not to Stalin *per se* but to the Soviet Union and socialism, for reasons that will be further elaborated.[4] It was rather the decisions taken after the death of Stalin and the consequent interplay of events that resulted in the alteration of the structure of authority in the communist movement.

Communist doctrine as the source of authority comes closer to the point, but it too is insufficient as an explanation of the source of authority. For doctrine, within limits, is what you make it. There is no fixed, unchanging set of beliefs to provide sure guidance to the individuals in a community. State farms are one day the supreme institutional form for the transition to communism; the next day they become coequal with collective farms. Ideology requires its interpreter. Was Trotsky less fit to interpret the ideology than Stalin, Mao Tse-tung than Khrushchev? Who conferred on Stalin in the fall of 1939 the right to label the war an imperialist war and consequently disgrace the Communists in countries threatened by the Axis Powers?

And conversely, what impelled the national communist leaderships to accept Stalin's dictum?

The authoritative person and the authoritative doctrine are derivatives of the charter of authority, so to speak, which emanates from Marxian ideas and values. These ideas constitute the source of authority which legitimatizes the exercise of power. Policy is accepted not merely because it is handed down by someone who stands in a position of power but because it purports to elaborate and concretize a body of thought—that is, a set of abstractions. Policy or action derived from a system of beliefs requires an interpreter who is clothed in authority, simply in order to prevent an unstructured response that would threaten the entire belief system. Thus ecclesiastical authority is related to its function of elaborating transcendental ideas. Authority in a political movement is analogous. For thirty-five years or more, the function of prescribing Marxian orthodoxy devolved on Lenin and his successors. The role of the ordinary individual committed to the belief system was to support the policy and action elaborated for the movement as a whole, which automatically became his own in the movement.

The source of authority in the international communist movement was the idea of World Revolution. World Revolution was the fundamental premise underlying the foundation of the Third (Communist) International, or Comintern. The "Manifesto"[5] issued by the first Congress of the Communist International made it plain that the International was destined to lead the way to world-wide proletarian revolution. Lenin in 1919 spoke of the victory of communism throughout the world, asserting it would not be long before a World Federal Republic of Soviets would be founded.[6] The idea of revolution was World Revolution, not the Bolshevik revolution in Russia. The latter was considered to be a happy accident. Premature in Marxian terms, the Bolshevik revolution could be "saved" only by revolution in the more advanced countries.

THE CONCEPT OF WORLD REVOLUTION

A distinction must be drawn between the meaning of World Revolution to the founders of the Comintern and the meaning the term has in common parlance. In contemporary usage, "World Revolution" is taken to mean any attempt by the Communists to extend their power. Under this definition, the subjugation of Eastern and Central Europe after World War Two was part of World Revolution. This is a perversion by both Communists and non-Communists of the Marxian concept of proletarian revolution. In the Marxian scheme, revolution was the inevitable product of the contradictions of capitalism which would produce a crisis-ridden, polarized society destined to be taken over by the proletariat from the bourgeoisie which had willy-nilly developed the instruments for its own destruction. Although Marx did not exclude conscious efforts at organization—indeed heightened consciousness and organization were effects of the developing crisis of capitalism—revolution was a function of the local socio-economic process. While the interests of the proletariat were international and while the proletariats of different countries might engage in mutual aid, revolution would be essentially a national affair. There was nothing to suggest the subordination of one party to another; indeed, as parties went, it was the German party that possessed the greatest prestige. In short, at the time of the establishment of the Comintern, the transcendent idea was that of World Revolution, in whose name policies were formulated, justified, and accepted. The phenomenon of revolution was world-wide in scope, subject everywhere to similar principles of political development and societal organization. The process of revolution in each state was natural and organic, having nothing to do (except in terms of atmospheric influence) with revolutionary developments in another state.

What basically altered the idea of World Revolution was not simply the fact of the Bolshevik revolution or the structuring by the Bolsheviks of the world revolutionary movement for their own purposes, but the palpable failure of revolution outside Russia and the manipulation of this dilemma by the Soviet leaders. If Marx's prognosis of revolution culminating in a proletarian seizure of power was based on a misreading of history, his adherents had obviously been led up the garden path. Whatever the virtues of Marx's analysis of capitalism, the course of events had suggested by 1917 (earlier, in fact) that the contradictions of capitalism would be ameliorated in ways other than through proletarian revolution. The German Socialist Party, for example, had been transformed—its theory aside—into a powerful but essentially politically reformist organization committed not only to the welfare of the working class but to the welfare of the population at large. Theories are notoriously resistant to facts. And in theory the proletarian revolution was yet to come in Germany—and elsewhere. But successful revolutions did not occur in Germany, or in Hungary, or in Austria. Two conclusions were possible: revolution in Europe was still premature but inevitable; or the theory of revolution was in want of alteration. The latter conclusion was most difficult for dedicated Socialists to accept. Time was on their side and they could still hasten the inevitable by working for it. But this is precisely what they did not do, because of the subtle transformation which the politics of the first communist state embroidered into the idea of World Revolution, thereby substituting a different set of values and a new concept of authority.

The failure of the communist parties to bring off a revolution was the decisive factor in shaping the future of the international communist movement. Conceivably, the movement could have continued as a loose organization with the Communist Party of the Soviet Union (CPSU) affiliated with it merely as one component of the world-wide structure (as indeed it was on paper). Or it could have excluded the CPSU as irrelevant to an organization whose main objective was the seizure of power. What it could not do and still survive as an organization dedicated to World Revolution was to tie itself to a communist party whose preoccupation with functioning as a state within an international system of states created for the Soviet Communists a different set of values.[7] Hence the entire history of the communist movement was conditioned by the Soviet leadership's constantly shifting doctrinal and policy postulates. The transcendent idea of World Revolution was debased, coming to mean only whatever suited the immediate policy interests of the USSR. Programmatic and institutional structures changed as circumstances required. The proletarian revolution in Russia came to represent the dictatorship of the state over and against the world communist revolution.

If World Revolution was the organizing principle of international communism, what then held the loyalty of members once this goal receded from the horizon and was manipulated in the interests of Soviet state power? In principle there was nothing to prevent the individual communist parties from going their separate ways. This option is now being exercised by a number of communist parties precisely when the power of the Soviet Union is at its zenith, but it appears to have been "unthinkable" in the early history of the movement. The explanations usually advanced are that the subservience of the parties is a product of Leninist concepts of organization, or that they were subject to the coercion of the Soviet leadership. At best the reasoning here is circular. Contrary to the notion that the early adherents of the Communist International surrendered their freedom to Lenin and his principles of party organization, they appear to have followed him with a spontaneity that is lacking in most organizations generally and was to disappear from the communist movement itself. Lenin had the ability to move individuals and masses and make them his unconditional followers. In Lenin there was uniquely linked the individual prestige of a charismatic personality with the authority of the idea of World Revolution. Lenin inspired a confidence which established his authority almost as an objective entity. But with the depersonal-

ization of the movement and its bureaucratization under Stalin, the individual member subordinated himself to the idea of the movement whose power was
exerted by the closest representative of this ideal force
—that is, the Soviet Union. Thus Stalin's power, unlike
Lenin's, did not flow from his individuality but rather
from the movement which gave authority to his decisions. It is therefore to the general nature of political
organization and to the particular values shared by
the membership rather than to a demonic concept of
organization that one must look for an explanation of
the cohesion of the communist movement.

THE MOVEMENT AND THE INDIVIDUAL

The relationship between the individual Communist
and the communist movement as a whole has most
frequently been characterized as *sui generis*. Theories
of totalitarianism have been elaborated and religious
parallels suggested to describe what has been considered to be a unique phenomenon. The atomization
of the individual member and his disciplined response
to all manner of policy seem to have required the development of new theories of behavior. Whatever the
validity of such theories to explain behavior within a
communist state—and this is not my concern here—
they are inadequate to explain the relationships between and within communist parties.[8] The error has
been, in my view, in transposing the potential for
violence at the disposal of the rulers of a communist
state to the movement at large. This is as a matter of
fact inaccurate and, on a more general level, a mis-

construal of the essence of authority. The leaders of the Communist International were able to exert their power because of the authority in which they were clothed, not vice versa. Authority devolved upon them precisely because of the regard in which they were held by the membership, not merely because they controlled the instruments of coercion. Coercion is a relative matter. Freedom of choice and response remains up to the point of the use of direct physical force. Freedom is self-restricted depending on the calculation of the consequences of disobedience. In general, acceptance of the norms of society places a restriction on certain acts which the individual might at times prefer. Acceptance of the basic values of the international communist movement likewise restricted behavior which Communists as individuals might have preferred. Individual Communists pooled their power to achieve a desired goal through the Communist International, which thus constituted approved power. As long as the desired goals were embodied in the International —and reasonable alternatives were seemingly lacking as the goals were subverted—the individual played out his role of active subordination.

Once the individual joins an organization, he has entered into a contractual relationship which, so to speak, exists over and above him. In so doing he subjects himself to norms different from those of his pre-induction behavior. The acts he performs are covered by his engaging in them as part of the organization. What he may do for his own gain or against his own inclinations is indiscriminately masked by the fact that he is doing it for the collectivity. He becomes part of the decisions taken, even against his convictions, because he is part of the organization; since he is responsible for the decision, he must act positively to support it without showing his dissent. As it becomes less possible for the individual to affect action taken on behalf of the collectivity, his response tends to become progressively automatic. His subordination to the leadership remains as a technical necessity to achieve the overriding goals. Progressive compromise of principle is thus a general law of organization and bureaucracy. It is no less so for a member of the communist movement. "Absorption in any group," Laski once wrote, "tends to mean narrowness instead of breadth, rigour instead of plasticity, unquestioning acceptance instead of enlightened agreement."[9]

The process is not, however, one of uncompensated depersonalization. In the very fact of participation in the general cause, the individual Communist transforms himself, adding something to his personality. While he is, on the one hand, depersonalizing himself within the organization, he achieves a special distinction in relation to those outside the circle of the initiated. This distinction was enhanced for the Communist by his association with the first revolutionary socialist state. The attraction of power, embodied in Soviet Russia, strongly reinforced the theoretical compulsion for remaining in the movement. The political idea had been translated into a political entity capable of exerting its influence on the world scene. There was pride in such attachment. A political nonentity leading an unimportant communist party becomes someone of consequence by virtue of his connection with the Soviet Union. He is taken seriously not merely by his party but also by his fellow countrymen, for whom he per-

sonifies Moscow's power locally. And of course there
are the normal bureaucratic reasons for maintaining
one's allegiance: power over people, perquisites of office, progressive inability to perform other work, etc.,
which need no elaboration.

In the interwar period, the communist party leaders,
lacking the direct administrative controls available in
a communist state, used the external source of authority
represented by Moscow to maintain their hold over the
parties. In coping with internal conflicts, they could
call in the authority of Moscow to maintain order.
Resort to external authority served as protection for
those already established in positions of power and
served to strengthen the centralized party structure
as well. Financial aid from the Soviet Union contributed to the welfare of the party, further increasing its
dependence on Moscow. Ties with Moscow were also
strengthened by the continuity of leadership in many
of the parties. (The leaders of the Italian Communist
Party in 1960, for example, were in general those who
reached the top levels of the party in the 1920s.) The
loyalty of party leaders to Moscow is not strictly a
function of a master-slave relationship; it should be
seen in the more positive sense as emanating from
leaders in their own parties who had an investment in
their past with all the psychological and political consequences that this implies.

Negative reasons also played their part in holding
the allegiance of the members. Where they had failed,
the Russian Communists had succeeded. Since they had
succeeded, they must possess certain keys to successful
revolution which others might emulate. Since the revolution was established in Russia, it had to be defended.

Not to defend it was by definition reactionary. There were no alternatives. Joining forces with the Socialist International was unthinkable after the great betrayal in 1914 when the socialist parties had voted to support their bourgeois governments. One could simply quit, but this would put one outside the realm of radical political action. Politics requires that choices be made, and what alternative radical movement existed that had already achieved the distinction of accomplishing its objective in one area or had the remotest chance of doing so?

THE EFFECT OF EXTERNAL PRESSURES

In addition to internal psychological and political factors, external circumstances helped shape the behavior patterns of the communist parties just as they did the development of "socialism in one country" in Russia. The failure of communist revolutions to materialize in Western and Central Europe decisively altered the orientation of the Bolshevik leaders in the direction of a nationalist and isolationist policy. A parallel development was the transfer of loyalty by the foreign Communists to Soviet Russia as *locum tenens* of World Revolution. The assurance of loyalty was reinforced by external pressure applied to Soviet Russia and by the repression of Communists in their respective countries. The attempts of the Great Powers after World War One to throttle the Bolshevik regime and, failing to do so, to isolate it, reduced communist freedom of choice and action. Though people are forgetful, there does not seem to be much doubt that the prevailing opinion of the Great Powers concurred with the late Winston Churchill's view that the revolutionary baby should have been strangled at birth. Intervention in Russia, including the participation of the United States, was anti-Bolshevik in purpose. This rather simple and understandable proposition has been obscured by various interpretations of the Entente's intervention as being for the sake of keeping Russia in the war, holding down German troops on the Eastern front, etc. No doubt these and other factors figured in the calculations, but the thrust was deeper and almost successful. That the foreign-supported civil war failed to depose the Bolsheviks was something of a miracle, so tenuous was Bolshevik authority. There is, moreover, a direct policy line from intervention to attempts to establish a *cordon sanitaire* around Soviet Russia, which even the defeated enemy, Germany, was asked to join as early as 1919 and which she declined to do. Negotiations leading up to the Genoa Conference in 1922 were a barely disguised attempt to seek a capitalist restoration in Russia by obtaining economic concessions, installing Western consortiums, and the like. Refusal to establish diplomatic relations and exclusion from the League of Nations were further attempts at isolation. Perhaps the best example of the deep and lingering hostility of the Western Powers to the Soviet Union in the interwar period was the failure to engage that country in the German-Czech crisis of 1938.

The intervention of the United States in 1918, ostensibly for the humanitarian purpose of freeing Czech prisoners of war to enable them to resume the fight against the Germans on the Western front and, more pointedly, to counterbalance the Japanese invasion of

Siberia was also, if less courageously defined, an attempt to support anti-Bolshevik forces.[10] Whatever
the ambiguity of American policy during the intervention, its hostility to the Bolshevik regime, manifested
by the presence of American troops in Siberia, and in
northern Russia, and its unwillingness to deal with the
Bolsheviks were the decisive factors, ideology aside, in
shaping the attitude of the Communists toward the
United States. The Bolshevik revolution in Russia implicitly threatened the social system of the Western
capitalist countries and in effect polarized the world.
To be sure, the two parts were of unequal magnitude,
scarcely requiring the degree of intense hostility en-
gendered in the West. Certainly Soviet Russia in 1917
—and even twenty years later—represented no military
threat to the Western Powers. Yet it was precisely the
social challenge of the new Marxist state which, warranted or not, provoked the active hostility of the West
and gave rise to a policy in the United States that was
conditioned more by ideology than by considerations
of actual power or national interest. Whether the Western Powers were correct in judging the new state as a
threat and in adopting the policies they did is immaterial for the argument here. The operative fact is that
they did so respond, placing Soviet Russia on the defensive and compelling an extraordinary loyalty on the
part of its supporters, for whom capitalism, symbol of
inequality, exploitation, and war, represented no alternative. The intervention in Russia, the blockade, and
anti-Bolshevik propaganda, often of hysterical proportions, constituted the objective ingredients of the communist doctrine of "capitalist encirclement." The ani-

mus toward the Bolshevik regime was reinforced by legal and administrative measures against the domestic communist movements. What may have appeared on the outside as an explosive situation marked by the attempt of the Bolshevik regime and its cohorts in non-communist countries to foment revolution appeared quite differently on the inside where the existence of the single socialist country appeared to be in danger of extinction together with the small and weak communist movements.[11] In the crisis so perceived, the priorities of revolution gave way to survival, and individual requirements gave way to protection of the indisputable achievements of the revolutionaries—that is, the first socialist state.

For many, the burgeoning dictatorship in Russia, the perversion of ideas, and the ruthlessness of policy were too much. But for those who remained loyal or who joined over the years, the Soviet Union represented the one hope in a world beset by economic depression, and by varieties of fascism in Western and Eastern Europe, Chiang Kai-shek-ism and imperialism in Asia. External pressure on Soviet Russia and the foreign Communists served to confirm the belief. They went along with Stalin not because of the mysterious workings of "Moscow domination" but for a variety of reasons, not the least of which was the pressure for solidarity imposed on them by anti-Soviet forces. The idea that communist (totalitarian) states require an artificially created external enemy to mobilize their populations is suspect; the external enemy exists as an objective reality which can, of course, be manipulated for internal purposes but scarcely requires fabrication.

THE CAUSES OF CHANGE

Nevertheless, the claim on men's loyalties must in time prove to be deserved. The goals for which men enter into certain relationships must be susceptible of achievement. Moreover, not all the members place identical values on the goals to be achieved; conflicting values constantly arise. In the communist movement there was most obviously a value conflict between the requirements of Soviet policy and the interests of the local communist parties. It is naïve to believe that the national party leaders had no political motive except the desire to submit to Moscow at whatever cost to themselves and to their parties. Communist leaders, too, are politicians, viewing their relations with Moscow in instrumental terms as a means of maximizing their personal power and the power of their parties. Their subordination to Moscow partakes of a complex process, but devotion to the idea of internationalism seems to have been one of the more important factors. Internationalism—a liberal ideal which looked toward the end of struggle between nations, of the oppression of one nation by another, and the emergence of a brotherhood of man—was taken over by the socialist movement, which added to the concept the abolition of private property as a necessary condition for the attainment of freedom and brotherhood. Socialism was then in essence an international idea dedicated to the creation of an economic and social order that would abolish national strife. While the Soviet Union did not correspond to an absolute internationalist's idea of internationalism, it was the nearest approach to socialism that there was. In the face of the obvious decline of internationalism with the increase of chauvinist nationalism after World War One, the Communists kept alive the idea of internationalism by drawing a strict line between day-to-day activity and the future socialist revolution. Practical activity was related to the ideal, however remotely.[12]

Primary loyalty, then, devolved upon the International—and on the Soviet Union so long as it could represent itself as the embodiment of internationalism —even to the exclusion of national communist interests. To reinforce the direction of loyalties, doctrines were redefined, ideas twisted, and institutions created to meet the changing conditions confronting the Soviet Union—not the Communist International. Not World Revolution but Sublimated or Suspended Revolution became the organizing principle; not active preparation for revolution but defense of the Soviet Union; not merely defense of the Soviet Union but defense of Stalin's variant of the Soviet Union. The international communist movement not only lost its purpose but became an instrument to defeat that purpose. The very tactics and stratagems it employed to conform to the decisions of the central apparatus weakened its potential as a revolutionary instrument. Stalin retained the formal apparatus largely for bureaucratic purposes: retention of the International was presumptive evidence that his elimination of the "Left Opposition" did not signify the abandonment of World Revolution. Leaders of various parties were useful to him in mobilizing pro-Soviet sentiment. Their existence was as much— or as little—justified as that of an international front organization to mobilize peace or women. Moreover, bureaucracies are by definition resistant to dissolution.

It is significant for understanding the communist loyalty pattern to note that the International was not shattered from within by those who wished to be free of Stalin's restrictive control, and that few attempts were made to set up a rival communist international. The psychological barrier to such action was clearly illustrated by the hesitations of Trotsky, ten years after Stalin's break with him, in organizing a Fourth International that would presumably take up where Lenin left off. Even then, Trotsky would not disown the USSR as the country of proletarian revolution. Rather, the International was dissolved from above, by Stalin in 1943 as a gesture of good will to his wartime allies. Actually, the International had long since ceased to be an effective organ of World Revolution, since Stalin had consistently used it for his own strictly national purposes, and its apparatus had, in any case, been decimated by that time by the Axis Powers. But the end of the Communist International was not the end of international communism. The pattern of loyalty survived World War Two and seemed to have achieved a permanent character. If, however, the international communist movement, considered as a well-defined, cohesive unit, is in difficulty today, it is precisely because it has not adapted itself rapidly and intelligently enough to change.

There is a presumption that the leaders of the national communist parties between the wars would have preferred a change in the structure of authority. Such an impression is conveyed by the occasional defections of important personages from the communist movement and by the activities of the Trotskyists. Yet, in the absence of authoritative data, together with the absence of a substantial record of behavior to the contrary, such a presumption may be in error. Not only were the members not ready to undertake the kind of action required to effect a different structure of authority, they may not have desired—or desired sufficiently—to do so. This is more than saying that they were unwilling to take the gamble; it means that they, unlike non-communist commentators, did not feel that the situation was sufficiently deplorable, or that the need for change was strong enough, or that their interests were sufficiently impinged upon, to attempt to force a change. It is a human enough trait to want to have more freedom of action in directing one's own (party's) affairs, but this is about as far as speculation can go. It was when the interests of particular units of the communist movement were more sharply affected, particularly when they became mass movements and began to exercise state power, that the Soviet Union began to suffer inroads into its authority.

Stalin made the error of supposing that authority was a fixed entity which did not have to be redefined and redetermined as circumstances changed. He expected obedience from Tito, and the record strongly affirmed that Stalin's orders would be obeyed. Disobedience is, however, recurrent in all authority structures, as any parent knows, and when the signal of revolt is sounded, the structure must be revised or it will become irrelevant. If there was anyone more surprised by his defiance of Stalin than Tito, it was Stalin. Similarly, the extent of the breakdown of Soviet authority over the communist movement must have come as a surprise to Khrushchev, whose innovations were, at best, designed to introduce a measure of flexibility into the system. He had "lost his authority" not because his formal position in the communist hierarchy had changed or because he had behaved in an un-Stalinesque manner, but because the environment had changed. His pronouncements had lost the authority they might have had some years back because opinions and values in the communist movement had changed, and the objective situation enabled the possessors of different views to translate them, at least partially, into action. Chinese Communist allegiance to the Soviet Union, seemingly permanent, was jeopardized because the Soviet world outlook did not appear to be working out effectively for the Chinese. The Albanian communist regime's subordination to the Soviet Union would not tolerate the suspicion of Yugoslavia's reassertion of control over Albania, as implied in the Tito-Khrushchev rapprochement. Allegiance in the international communist movement, as in other political movements, depends in the long run on what the members get out of it. Unity is preferable to disunity; hence subordination to preserve order. But this subordination must fill the needs of the subordinated as external circumstances change.

The foregoing remarks on the structure of authority merely serve to recall that the international communist movement, like other political movements, has been subject to change. Values, goals, authority, and institutions have all undergone transformation. Whatever influence origin and development may exert on the future configuration of communism, it is not amiss to stress the idea of change and development as a counter to the usual static constructs of communism. This is not to deny that a convincing model of communist behavior, say, under Stalin in the 1930s, could be constructed; merely to argue that this was only one phase —a long and important one to be sure—of a development that has not been unilinear. Moreover, since grown organisms never quite escape their early conditioning, it is perhaps useful to recall the premises on which the movement was founded. The next chapter, therefore, attempts to provide a rough outline of the changes that have taken place in the pattern of authority and control in the international communist movement.

2. CHANGES IN THE PATTERN OF AUTHORITY AND CONTROL

The most obvious characteristic of the change in authority and control in the communist movement is the absence since 1943 of a formal international organization as a guiding mechanism.[1] If the present breakdown in the authority of the movement could be ascribed merely to the absence of such an organization, the problem of analysis would be simplified. But such is not the case. The cohesion of the movement was maintained under Stalin both with and without the existence of the Comintern. Paradoxically, the practices developed during the Comintern period establishing norms of expected behavior, whether prescribed or proscribed, facilitated the cohesion of the movement after the organization was scuttled. But even these tried and true institutions have proved to be inadequate to cope with the new situation in which communism found itself after World War Two.

A schema of changes in the structure of authority and control in the communist movement runs immediately into the obstacle of the inadequacy of nomenclature and taxonomy for political organization, especially international political organization. It is suggestive to describe, as Duverger has, the relationship between an individual communist party and the International as having the characteristics of "autocracy," especially in contrast to the relationship of the socialist parties to the Second International.[2] However, as he qualifies it, the degree of autocracy diminishes in relation to the extent to which the authority of the Russians is recognized. Since this is precisely the relationship which has changed over the years for one reason or another, and the one on the basis of which a schema is being drawn up, it is difficult to assign any generally relevant terminology to the various phases. Instead, the terminology used is intended here merely to highlight phases in the development of international communism and should not be interpreted in terms of the American political scene.

VOLUNTARY ASSOCIATION FOR WORLD REVOLUTION—1919–1928

The general purpose behind the foundation of the Communist International was to join forces for World Revolution. The immediate purpose was to prevent the Second International from reconstituting itself as the authorized spokesman for international socialism.[3] The parties affiliated with the Socialist International had, in Lenin's view, betrayed the cause of socialism by supporting the war waged by their respective countries, in spite of their pledges not to do so. In a statement issued as early as November 1914,[4] through the anti-war socialist meetings at Zimmerwald (September 5–8, 1915) and Kienthal (April 1916), the Bolsheviks attempted to lay the groundwork for a new revolutionary international composed of various left wing and anti-war groups. Not until March 1919, after the Bolshevik revolution, were they successful in doing so.

The organization of the Comintern took place at a time when world revolutionary hopes ran high and when the Bolsheviks, on their own showing, admitted to the precarious nature of their own revolution. Revolution had to occur in the West, particularly in Germany, to "save" the Russian revolution. This notion was derived from the circumstances that the revolution had occurred in a country which did not possess the Marxian prerequisites for revolution. There was therefore a comity of interests between the Bolsheviks and the Western European Communists. Both were committed to revolution and their interests were reciprocal. The delegates, assembled with difficulty in the midst of war-disrupted communication, were not particularly impressive or representative of the socialist movement as a whole. Since the majority of the delegates were emigrés who happened to be in Russia, it is often concluded that the Comintern was a put-up job, the delegates merely rubber-stamping Lenin's decision. But reading backwards in history is dangerous. No group at that time was more dedicated than the Bolsheviks to the notion of equality within the movement. Whatever the circumstances, the delegates had come together representing, legally or not, independent groups bound by their antagonism to the war (and to the international socialist movement which was involved in the war) and by their revolutionary proclivities. The relational atmosphere is conveyed by Lenin's reluctance to ride roughshod over the German Eberlein, who arrived with instructions to oppose the foundation of an international as premature.[5] The new international, in the characteristic outlook of the German Social Democratic Party, was to await the formation of mass revolutionary parties. Socialist organization should proceed from below and not from above. To Lenin the issue was tactical—that is, the problem was not one of establishing an organization under Russian tutelage, but rather that of establishing an organization at once. Although he pressed for immediate action, he was nevertheless willing for the sake of unity to postpone the foundation of the international. He had his way because of the fortuitous arrival of the Austrian Steinhardt, who brought with him news that fed the hope of imminent European revolution and who pleaded for the constitution of a revolutionary international. The delegates went along with him, Eberlein abstaining. Thus the organizational meeting, which had seemed destined merely to choose a committee to formulate its rules, emerged as the First Congress of the Communist International by an act of the general will.

If the *ad hoc* and unrepresentative nature of the organizational meeting suggests that the International was nothing but a Bolshevik show, the Second Congress of the Comintern should dispel this notion. It was this Congress, attended by more than two hundred delegates representing about thirty-five countries, "a large percentage of them . . . legitimate spokesmen for existing groups in various countries,"[6] which accepted the "Twenty-One Conditions of Affiliation" together with the Statutes, which, with some amendments in 1928, were to govern the Comintern. These were designed to forge a unified, independent, international, revolutionary organization on the Bolshevik model. The International was not conceived, in Trotsky's words, as the "simple arithmetical sum of all the labor and socialist associations existing in various countries" but as the "Communist Party of the international proletariat."[7] Scorning socialist and bourgeois critics who charged that Moscow was confronting the parties with dictatorial demands through the exaction of conditions of affiliation, Trotsky asserted that "by joining the ranks of the Third International, an organization of a given country not only becomes subordinate to the common, vigilant and exacting leadership, but it itself acquires the right to actively participate in the leadership of all other sections of the Communist International."[8] What Trotsky apparently had in mind was the play of reciprocal relations among independent communist parties acting in strict unison to carry out revolutionary objectives—what may be called Leninist (to distinguish it from Stalinist) democratic centralism on an international level. What Trotsky certainly did not have in mind was an organization dictated to by Moscow. The flavor of the times may be appreciated in Trotsky's comments on the headquarters of the Comintern, which were located in Moscow, perhaps temporarily, until the revolution moved westward. He wrote in the spring of 1919:

The revolutionary "primogeniture" of the Russian proletariat is only temporary. . . . If today the center of the Third International lies in Moscow—and of this we are profoundly convinced—then on the morrow this center will shift westward: to Berlin, to Paris, to London. However joyously the Russian proletariat has greeted the representatives of the world working class within the Kremlin walls, it will with an even greater joy send its representatives to the Second Congress of the Communist International in one of the Western European capitals. For a World Communist Congress in Berlin or Paris would signify the complete triumph of the proletarian revolution in Europe and consequently throughout the world.[9]

The Russians had a special position in the Comintern from the outset. Given the circumstances, this was as normal a situation as any that might take place when one association takes the initiative in forming a larger association. It is obvious, as Friedrich remarked in another but pertinent context, that ". . . founding the political order is related to political leadership."[10] Although the behavior of the Socialist International with regard to the war came in for criticism among Socialists, disenchantment was by no means so widespread as to foreclose its reconstitution after the war with its national affiliates substantially intact. The formation of another revolutionary international, that is, was not inevitable. Just as the decision to seize power in Russia was almost solely Lenin's, so the decision to found the Third International in 1919 was basically his. To him and his party went the prestige and authority of the founding act. It seems quite natural under the circumstances for the foreign communist parties and groups to have looked to the Bolsheviks for guidance and

for help.[11] The Russian Party, as the founding party—
and the only one at that time of wartime disruption—
possessed the authority to make rules for the entire
movement. Authority is indispensable in any political
organization—let alone one geared to revolutionary action—and the largest and best-organized of the existing
organizations is commonly recognized as the appropriate body to make rules for all the components.[12] If the
participating organizations objected to the rules, they
could get out—or be forced out, as Lenin indeed
wanted them to be. Nevertheless, the special position
occupied by the Russians did not mean, nor was it
meant to mean, that the Comintern would be a Rus-
sian-dictated affair or an organization operating in the
exclusive interests of Soviet Russia, even if certain
Russian Communists felt they were possessed of superior wisdom. Rather, it was dedicated, by pronouncement as well as by what can be determined from the
early behavior of the Bolsheviks, to World Revolution
—that is, to the interests of all revolutionaries.

In spite of Russia's special position in the Comintern,
decision-making was designed to be "consensual."
"Democratic centralism," as the operating organizational principle, originally meant that decisions would
be arrived at through common consent and would then
become absolutely binding on the membership. This
concept presupposed freedom of discussion among the
membership and the availability to the executive organs of rank-and-file opinion before decisions were
made. On the other hand, decisions, once made with
rank-and-file participation in the process, would become binding on the movement. The system would be
centralized but democratic through the participation

of the membership in discussion and application of decisions. Agreement through this form of consensual process seemed at the time to be eminently workable because of the common theoretical orientation and common revolutionary interests of the members.

Expressed in organizational terms, the national communist parties were represented in a policy-making body in which the Russians had a weighted but by no means preponderant vote. (They had, for example, five of eighteen seats in the Executive Committee of the Comintern in 1922.) Representation on the basis of one vote for each constituent member may be the democratic optimum, but it is by no means the proved desideratum in political association, nor is it necessarily the most democratic form of organization in relation to the burden of responsibility. Soviet dictatorship over the Comintern developed not as a function of the character of the organization as such, or through weighted voting procedures, but rather through the acquiescence of the parties at large to a shifting of priorities which saw world-revolutionary goals eclipsed by reasons of state.

Capitulation to German terms for peace at Brest Litovsk in 1918 provoked the Bolsheviks into an awareness that their existence might depend more on the maintenance of a state within a hostile system of states than on the spread of revolution. But this awareness grew slowly. Incompatibility between the interests of World Revolution and Russian policy was not conceded, and if it was perceived the perception did not for some time attain the level of conscious purposefulness. The Bolsheviks at the time failed to accept the dichotomy between World Revolution and *raison d'état*.

Their failure, or psychological inability, to perceive this dichotomy is qualitatively different from the later proposition that the interests of World Revolution are equivalent to those of Soviet Russia. The pledge in "The Twenty-One Conditions" to protect the "Soviet Republics"—quite natural—is of a different order from the acceptance of any act of the Soviet Union as an organic part of the world-revolutionary struggle.

This unresolved duality of commitment is substantially documented in the early history of the movement. In signing the Rapallo treaty with Germany in April 1922, for example, the Bolshevik state had been able to break out of the isolation imposed upon it by the Entente Powers. Germany was the linchpin of Soviet policy in the twenties. Yet it was revolution in Germany that preoccupied the Comintern during this period—that is, the overthrow of the very state on which the Bolsheviks were basing their policy. That no state would brook the serious possibility of subversion at the hands of another—and in this case friendly—state did not deter the Bolsheviks, for whom the realities of relations between states had not yet fully struck home. To take but one other example, the prescription for revolution in the colonial areas was complicated by the desire to do something immediately to weaken the power of the European states which had holdings on Russia's borders. The strategy advocated in the Comintern by M. N. Roy was uncompromisingly revolutionary, directed at both the native bourgeoisie and the metropolitan power (colonial or imperial), led by Communists and aimed at seizing power. Lenin's preference was a strategy directed against the metropolitan powers led by the native bourgeoisie and backed by the Communists, putting the latter in a position of supporting a liberating but nevertheless bourgeois movement. Reconciliation of Lenin's and Roy's positions was effected by *calling* the strategy "national revolutionary"—national (Lenin), revolutionary (Roy)—and stipulating that the Communists should support only those bourgeois movements which would permit the communist movement to carry on an independent existence. Reconciliation of the two positions, that is, could be effected only on paper. Once the interests of the Soviet state intruded on Comintern policy, World Revolution in its Marxian context—and even in its pre-World War One Leninist version—became obsolete. What followed was the progressively rationalized formula that what promoted the interests of the USSR by that very token promoted the interests of World Revolution. Acceptance of this rationalization was tantamount to a perversion of the values of the revolutionary communist movement. The consequence was a moral deterioration in which principles were progressively whittled away, so that all that was left to the foreign Communists, given their political weakness, was to accept Soviet demands without question or get out. Organizational subservience to Moscow followed. The logic of the foreign Communists' abdication of principle implied the acceptance of the organizational devices imposed upon them.

THE AUTOCRATIC CENTRALIST ORGANIZATION, 1928–1956

The transformation of the Comintern from a voluntary association of equals into an appendage of CPSU policy and finally into an instrument of Stalin's personal rule began before 1928 but is conveniently associated with the Sixth Comintern Congress, held in that year. As the Executive Committee of the Communist International (ECCI) progressively increased its power after 1922, in effect assuming the prerogatives reserved for the Congresses, the democratic character of the association appeared to be preserved by representation on the ECCI from the various communist parties. Policy direction, theoretically, would derive from the consensus of an international collegium drawn from the communist movement. But circumstances conspired to have it otherwise. The dimming of revolutionary prospects required the formulation of new strategy and tactics. Lenin's death in 1924 provoked a struggle for power in the Soviet Union, which, since it involved questions of theory and orientation, implicated the Comintern. Moreover, his death deprived the communist movement of that element of common sense which had already called attention to the fact that Russification was not an answer to the Comintern's problems.

Organizationally, the parties yielded to the policy of cooptation of members of the "Enlarged ECCI," which substituted itself for the Congresses and, in fact, came to be dominated by a small inner group called the Political Secretariat. Soviet control over the Comintern finally came to be exercised through the Political Secretariat, buttressed by the interlocking functions between Soviet party and state organs, including the secret police and the intelligence apparatus on the one hand and the Comintern apparatus on the other. Direct administrative control over the national parties was extended by a number of devices. For example, the Third Comintern Congress adopted the principle of "dual subordination" of the parties, meaning that they would be responsible both to their national congresses and to the ECCI. In practice, the authority of the ECCI came to overshadow that of the national congresses.

The Sixth Congress enlarged and formalized the authority of the central apparatus. All ECCI decisions were declared binding on the national parties. All national party programs had to be endorsed by the ECCI; directives from the ECCI to the national parties were to be given immediate implementation; the ECCI had the power to expel either whole parties or individual members of national parties; and a large international apparatus was constructed, complete with field bureaus, Comintern representatives, instructors, couriers, and more. This aspect of the communist movement's history has been told many times and needs no amplification. What should be emphasized, however, is that the communist parties and the membership cooperated in this *Gleichschaltung*; even certain of the national party leaders who dropped out at this time would surely have remained had they succeeded in retaining their positions of power.

The so-called bolshevization—or bureaucratization—of the Comintern, then, centralized the world communist movement and welded it into a responsive instrument of Soviet policy. Stalin's consolidation of internal power was accompanied by the extension of his control over the Comintern. Whatever collective debate and collegial rule remained was progressively eliminated. The Comintern became an instrument of Stalin's personal dictatorship.

The surrender of the communist parties on counts

of both theory and organizational principle was underscored at the Sixth Congress. In 1928 it embarked on
an ultra-left policy in conjunction with Stalin's launch-
ing of the First Five Year Plan and his purge of the
"Right Opposition." Neither the motive of policy orientation nor the capabilities of the parties (except,
perhaps, in Germany, and there a more moderate col-
laborative policy with the Socialists might have paid
off) had anything to do with revolution, the Program
of the Sixth Congress to the contrary notwithstanding.
Stalin's leftist international policy may be characterized
as a rear guard action to "cover" his plunge into national construction (socialism in one country) and as
a device to demonstrate Stalin's ostensible continued
interest in World Revolution. Although in retrospect
the revolutionary program of the Sixth Congress may
still strike one, to some extent, as an inexplicable
policy because it was sure to antagonize foreign governments precisely when Stalin was looking for their
assistance, or at least their tolerance,[13] surely the Trotskyists were correct in labeling it merely as an ideological cover for the abandonment of revolutionary
internationalism in favor of a nationalist policy. As a
former Trotskyist put it, "If the gist of the dispute that
split the Third (Communist) International had to be
stated in the tersest and bluntest formula, no more
accurate one could be found than 'nationalism vs. internationalism.' "[14]

But this was not all. Stalin had little confidence in
the foreign Communists. Control over the communist
parties was exercised less through the Comintern than
through his trusted emissaries. The purges inside Russia

in the thirties were accompanied by purges of the Comintern personnel. Leadership of the communist parties was determined by willingness to accept and approve the recurrent changes in the groupings of the central apparatus. What with the decimation of the Comintern apparatus in the Far East and Germany and the purging of the personnel, the Comintern was for all practical purposes an empty organization at the end of the thirties.

Paradoxically, it was after the parties had been bolshevized and had accepted regimentation to the point where the Comintern was dispensable that a turn in Soviet foreign policy revitalized them politically. Soviet collective security policy against fascism was complemented by the Popular Front policy of the communist parties. The gambit of cooperation with the socialist and bourgeois parties required that the communist parties be given a greater measure of tactical autonomy. Associated with a popular cause, the parties increased their membership and political influence and, except for the period of the Nazi-Soviet Pact, continued to gain throughout the war, with the result that certain parties—such as the French and Italian—grew into mass movements. As M. N. Roy has pointed out,[15] the Popular Front movement deviated from the original position of the Communist International on both organizational and theoretical counts, thus taking another step toward the eventual dissolution of the latter body.

The Comintern was dissolved in May 1943, as a foreign-policy move to placate the USSR's wartime allies, most probably as a conciliatory gesture to President Roosevelt. In dissolving it, Stalin did not sacrifice much of substance, as the foregoing discussion should indicate. The statement explaining the dissolution declared, with a greater measure of truth than was intended, that the Comintern had ceased to be useful and had even become a hindrance to the development of the parties. It pointed out that even before the war a contradiction had appeared between the international directing center and the parties in countries which were experiencing fundamentally different paths of development and that, moreover, the parties were "mature" enough to function without benefit of a directing center.[16] "Maturity" here meant that agencies of control had been so perfected that Stalin could depend on the reliability of the parties. Direct administrative controls and day-to-day management could be dispensed with because patterns of obedience had been learned. (A central, if not international, mechanism did exist in the CPSU Central Committee, though this fact was of course not pointed out.) The supreme behavioral principle was embodied in the concept of "proletarian internationalism," which, according to Stalin, meant unconditional support of the Soviet Union. Stalin's version of "proletarian internationalism" marks the length of the road to authoritarianism traveled by the communist movement when it is contrasted with Lenin's at the Second Comintern Congress:

> . . . *Proletarian internationalism demands, firstly, that the interests of the proletarian struggle in one country be subordinated to the interests of the proletarian struggle on a world scale, and, secondly, that a nation which is achieving victory over the bourgeoisie*

be able and willing to make the greatest national sacri-
fices for the sake of overthrowing international capital.[17]

The mechanics of proletarian internationalism—or
how to know how to defend the interests of the Soviet
Union—were a fairly simple proposition. Communication among Communists had been developed to the
point where the "line" could be transmitted through
key Soviet pronouncements in speeches, newspapers,
theoretical journals, etc. The fact that these could also
be read by non-Communists was immaterial: Communists do not deign to conceal their aims, they say. Party
congresses, exchange of delegations, CPSU emissaries,
financial subsidy, etc., all contributed to the coordi-
nating process. But the war did serve to disrupt communications with Moscow, and, as the United States
and the USSR decided to test each other in Europe,
Stalin created a limited organization called the Information Bureau of Communist and Workers' Parties,
better known as the Cominform. With membership
from the communist parties of Eastern and Central Europe and the mass communist parties of France and
Italy, Stalin ostensibly hoped to tighten control over the
new communist states, for one, and to thwart American
policy aimed at rehabilitating and revitalizing Western Europe. As a control organ for these important
parties, the Cominform automatically served as a pol-
icy- and doctrine-disseminating center for all communist parties.

Whatever plans Stalin may have had to expand the
Cominform into an organization of all communist
parties—and there is very little evidence to document

his intention—were aborted by Tito's assertion of independence. The Cominform's expulsion of Yugoslavia in 1948 was its last act; it existed subsequently through the medium of its journal, *For a Lasting Peace, for a Peoples' Democracy!*, transferred from Belgrade to Bucharest, until it was formerly dissolved by Khrushchev in 1956.

Tito's defection from the Soviet orbit spelled the end of international communism as a cohesive movement controlled by Moscow. The monolithic character of the movement was shattered, but this did not result, as it did later with the defection of the Chinese Communists, in "bicentrism"—that is, in a rival party actively holding itself out as a center of authority. What effect Tito's defiance of Moscow had on other parties and their desire to emulate him is not a matter of clear record. The expulsion of Yugoslavia from the Cominform seemingly did not affect Stalin's control over the European state parties. His control was direct, making control through the medium of the Cominform superfluous. The weakness of the national communist leaderships with respect to their own populations, and their dependence on the Soviet Union at that time, tied them absolutely to Stalin. Insurance of his control over the satellite parties was doubled by a series of purges in the wake of the Titoist defection.

Moscow's control over the communist movement outside Eastern Europe seemed, however, to be less secure than in the interwar period, though this conclusion can only be advanced tenuously because of lack of information. It is known, however, that the Japanese and Indian parties, directed by Moscow to shift their strategies, accomplished this only after considerable factional strife.[18] The expulsion from the Swiss Communist Party of its old leader, Nicole, was accomplished in circumstances which suggested that Moscow was not quite in control of the situation. China, of course, is another matter.

Stalin's death in 1953 did not in itself alter the allegiance of the communist movement to Moscow. The national communist parties had submitted to Stalin's personal rule because their allegiance belonged to the CPSU and the USSR as the incarnation of World Revolution. This was as true for those parties which had developed a mass following on the basis of anti-fascism both before and during World War Two as for the others—most in fact—whose roots in the national life were so tenuous that they had no reason for existing apart from their devotion to the Soviet Union. Nevertheless, the struggle for power within the Soviet Union after Stalin's death, the new international environment, and finally the positions of power which certain of the communist parties achieved in their own countries combined to set the communist movement off on new roads.

DECENTRALIZATION, 1956–

The present period may be characterized as "polycentric" for no other reason than that a single center of authority no longer exists in the international communist movement.[19] Various communist parties, professing their allegiance to Marxism-Leninism and to the cause of the international proletariat, have refused to take direction from Moscow. This, to an outside observer, spells the doom of the international communist movement considered as a cohesive body acting in concert to achieve agreed-upon objectives. For the communist insider, however, nothing has happened to the movement *qua* movement. All the dissident parties consider themselves to be part of the international movement, are conducting their opposition from within the movement, and profess to object only to Soviet dictation. Division in the movement is caused by the refusal to abide by Stalin's version of proletarian internationalism, which in essence, if not in detail, was carried into the post-Stalin period. Re-establishment of unity, however, presupposes concessions to the dissenting parties which would result in the institutionalization of polycentrism—that is, Soviet acceptance of the independence and autonomy on various levels of the communist parties.[20] *De facto* recognition of the independence of the parties, however, would probably accelerate centrifugal tendencies and national separatism and the erosion of ideological precepts conceived for the seizure of power and the construction of socialism and communism. In short, the structure of authority and control has broken down; the present period is characterized by the search to re-establish unity on the basis of proletarian internationalism's being given a new context and, failing that, the acceptance of independent communist parties and states.

Khrushchev took the initiative in redefining the nature of relations between the parties and in so doing contributed to the divisive forces in the movement. In attempting to repair the break between Yugoslavia and the Soviet Union, Khrushchev made a virtue of necessity by recognizing the multiplicity of forms of socialist development and drawing the conclusion that relations between the two countries must be conducted on the basis of "mutual respect for, and non-interference in, internal affairs for any reason whatsoever."[21] The principle of equality between communist countries—and parties—once established in the Yugoslav case, could not be denied to the others. The Polish Communists were the first to put the concept to the test by installing Gomulka in power over the objections and fears of the Soviet leaders. To various degrees, other communist parties have put substance into the concept by exercising their independence insofar as their local conditions and inclinations would allow. As a result many centers have sprung up, in the sense that certain parties—the Chinese, Albanian, Yugoslav, New Zealand, and others —are making their decisions independently of Moscow. On the other hand, polycentrism in the sense that there is more than one center for the direction of the international communist movement does not properly exist; the situation rather is that Moscow is attempting to restore its role as the leader of international communism—and Peking is challenging it.

In seeking to restore its authority, Moscow has been forced to accept the equality of the parties as a datum rather than as a manipulative device to be applied differently to different situations. Specifically, the Soviet leaders advocated at the Moscow Conference of Representatives of Workers and Communist Parties (November 10–December 1, 1960) that the principle of majority rule should prevail in resolving interparty disputes.[22] That Moscow still could count on the support of a majority of parties no doubt helped it take the plunge into the democratic method. Moreover, on the principle of democratic centralism, the majority vote would be a binding obligation for all communist parties. Insofar as their place in the movement was concerned, the Soviet leaders stated that they no longer wished to be called "head" of the movement, but they sought to have their primacy acknowledged by having the Conference endorse the decisions of the Twentieth (1956) and Twenty-first (1959) CPSU Congresses, which, among others, laid down the general line for the communist parties.

The Chinese Communists too proceeded from the proposition of the equality of parties. They refused to accept Moscow's democratic alternative on the ground that they would be bound by an "arithmetical majority" —that is, votes at the disposal of Moscow. Democratic centralism was fine within parties, according to the Chinese position, but not between sovereign and independent parties. Decisions should be made on the basis of "unanimity through consultation." The Chinese, moreover, asserted that the decisions of CPSU congresses could not be binding on other parties and reserved the right to criticize international communist policy. In effect, the Chinese argued for the right of veto, implicitly asserting the right of any party to pursue its policy regardless of Moscow's wishes or the majority opinion taken at communist meetings. All the Conference could do was to state that decisions should be taken jointly through bilateral or multilateral meetings.

The failure to come to agreement at the Moscow meeting dramatically illustrated the erosion of Moscow's authority in the movement. Underlying the disagreement is the conflict over goals and policies, which reflects the particularist ambitions of the various parties.

Having rejected the principle of dictatorial dispensation, the communist parties now employ their heritage of Marxism-Leninism as a disruptive force, in precisely the opposite function from that it was supposed to perform. There is no unity because the various parties read into the abstractions and contradictions of the doctrine only those precepts on which they base their own policies. Nationalism and particularism have taken command of the communist movement.

3. THE DEVELOPMENT
OF POLYCENTRISM

Myths are as much the reality of politics as the so-called objective factors of geography and environment. Socialist internationalism, the new international brotherhood of man, succumbed to the pressures of social patriotism in 1914. Dead for all to see, it was yet resurrected in the cause of communist internationalism, which, in turn, died aborning in the 1920s. In an artificial state, it existed in the form of Stalinist internationalism, a sort of Soviet patriotism once removed, until that too foundered on the rock of nationalism. Yet both the Soviet and the Chinese Communists are loath to concede the condition and continue to voice their appeals in the name of internationalism, unity, and solidarity.

RESURGENCE OF NATIONALISM

Of all the underlying factors which have contributed to the polycentric phase of the communist movement,

nationalism, a reactionary force in the communist lexi-
con, has figured most decisively. This is a term whose
general import is clear enough but whose specific
meaning, under the microscope of analysis, eludes precise definition. For the purpose at hand, nationalism
may be thought of as the attempt to achieve and safeguard the integrity of a communist state or a communist
party against the requirements of an overriding communist internationalism defined heretofore, at least, by
the Soviet Union. Thus perceived, the nationalism of
the communist states is similar to the traditional nationalism of the Western state system, although the
Communists still profess internationalism as a higher
loyalty. The communist parties out of power, in order
to cope more effectively with local conditions, exhibit
nationalism as a form of particularism. The expression
of nationalism has, of course, varied from communist
party to communist party, depending upon the particular conditions of the area. In each instance it has been
bound up with the will to power and the particular
ambitions of individuals. As with traditional nationalism, historical conditions and national character have
played a role—witness the Polish popular support of
Gomulka in his confrontation with the Russians in
1956. Geographical circumstances were significant factors for Yugoslavia and Albania. Special foreign-policy
interests have conditioned the responses of the Chinese
Communist Party, and the defense of economic integrity has found the Rumanian Communist Party defying
Soviet attempts at international economic integration.
Of the communist parties out of power, the Italian
Communist Party has devised within the framework
of the constitutional system a program of "structural

reform" that bears a closer resemblance to the orientation of a democratic socialist party than to that of a
communist party. While the precise and operative
causal sequence that has brought the international communist movement to its present parlous state must be
left to the labors of the historians, it seems clear that
the phenomenon of nationalism has put an end to "international proletarian solidarity"—Stalin style.

Since World War Two the general resurgence of
nationalism—let alone General de Gaulle—has made it
somewhat easier, despite current mythology, to accept
the fact that monolithic communism as it appeared
under Stalin's rule was subject to the same divisive
forces which disrupted the non-communist world. If
internationalism symbolizes a higher stage of man's
political development, in which he is free from manipulation for the special interests of the state, it is nevertheless a symbol that commands little of the loyalty of
mankind. That the Soviet Union was able for so long
to profit from the idea of internationalism, even in a
perverted form, testifies to the power of the idea of
revolutionary Marxism in a world committed to pragmatism and approved change. In retrospect, communist
internationalism appears to have congealed at an early
stage and to have managed to survive precisely in the
guise of Soviet patriotism through the manipulation of
symbols that became progressively weaker. It was,
moreover, sheer chance that the phenomenon lasted as
long as it did. The rise of fascism in the thirties imbued
the communist parties with a new *élan* and gave them
the opportunity to rebuild their memberships. World
War Two froze the relations between the parties and
Moscow and again provided the parties with the op-

portunity to increase their influence. The politico-military events of World War Two shaped the situation which resulted in the establishment of communist states in Europe and Asia. History had not in fact predicted; communism expanded through the fortunes of war, diplomatic bargaining (or bungling, some would say), and the efforts of communist parties in countries where traditional parties had abdicated or had become tainted. Communism expanded but it had become more diffuse. Conflict of interest was bound to occur in areas which had spawned large parties or in which Communists controlled the state.

The expectations of Stalinist internationalism were not altered by the attachment to the communist movement after World War Two of a number of communist states.[1] The nature of the problems affecting the movement had changed but not the performance principle of the communist parties. The communist state parties were charged with the task of creating the prerequisites for the construction of socialism along lines prescribed by Moscow. Institutions were devised for common application—such as the "Peoples' Democracies," communist-controlled governments performing the function of the dictatorship of the proletariat. Programs of industrialization and agricultural collectivization were inaugurated to follow the trail blazed by the Soviet Union. The new states were spared the problems of foreign policy, which, by definition, fell to the USSR as leader of the camp.

This exercise in *Gleichschaltung* was based on a number of assumptions which in retrospect appear false but which at the time appeared plausible.[2] In the first place it was assumed that ideology would serve as a cohesive force and would furnish the guidelines for the new states. Implicit was the assumption that the authority of the Soviet Union as arbiter and dispenser of the doctrine would remain unchallenged. These assumptions ignored the fact that ideology merely provides a general framework within which particular policy choices can be made. For example, ideology provides no guidance as to whether to aid Egypt's economy. More to the point, it does not answer such questions as whether state ownership of farms or cooperative ownership is the proper institution for the development of a communist society. Ideology is a cohesive force only so long as there is a consensus, which implies that it meets the basic, and changing, requirements of the followers. Contrary to most opinion, ideology under Stalin in the forties was relatively unimportant—that is to say, it was less important than in the twenties and after the death of Stalin—because it was frozen; it was largely ukase. One consequence of this situation was the erosion of ideology in the movement; the members were Communists but anything but True Believers.

Another assumption which proved false was that what had been accomplished in the Soviet Union could be accomplished in the other communist states. The countries could be industrialized, agriculture collectivized, class structure atomized, all toward the building of a society with "socialist" values. Although Soviet society is far from having achieved these goals, at least it has had forty-five years to develop some lasting institutions. A similar development might have taken place in the other communist countries, but the Communists were working against time—that is, against the resistance to the imposition of foreign control and manners which seems to rise automatically and to be reinforced by traditional cultural patterns. History, contrary to a cherished communist belief, did not prove to be working in the interests of communism in Eastern and Central Europe.

Finally, the expectation that the primary allegiance of the communist leaders would be to the Soviet Union has proved to be misplaced. This is not to say that all or most communist leaders look first and foremost to their own interests. But many leaders are looking more to the interests of their own parties, particularly in domestic affairs, and have in fact developed a considerable area of autonomy in putting through policies which are frowned upon by the Soviet leaders. ("Structural reform" in Italy, for example, is much too revisionist for the taste of the CPSU.) Some have even declared their outright opposition to and independence of the Soviet Union on foreign as well as domestic policy. In other words, the response of the communist leaders to changing conditions and to positions of power and responsibility has been a weakening of their allegiance to Stalinist-type internationalism. They still profess allegiance to internationalism, but the content of the word has changed along with their changing outlook. The internationalism of the Yugoslavs and that of the Chinese, for example, differ from each other and the internationalism of both differs from the Soviet. It is almost as if the Soviet leaders, operating on the assumptions of an ideal internationalism of the twenty-first century, were caught up in an outbreak of nineteenth-century nationalism.

THE NEW COMMUNIST COUNTRIES

In terms of Soviet direction of the international communist movement—the problem of authority and control—the establishment of a dozen communist countries after World War Two qualitatively changed the nature of the movement. It was one thing to coordinate the strategies of communist parties, most of which were weak and in opposition to established governments; it was quite another to coordinate social revolution in communist countries with different socio-economic structures, customs, prejudices, and so on. Not only were the problems of another order, but the stakes were enormously higher. Yet the institutions of control that obtained before the war were automatically expected to cope with the new environment. The leaders of the communist countries were regarded by both the communist and the non-communist population as members of the international communist staff, acting in trust, as it were, for the Soviet Union. This arrangement presupposed that direct administrative controls and coercion could be exerted for a sufficiently long period of time to transform the social structure and secure the loyalty or acquiescence of the population, as happened in the Soviet Union. The arrangement also presupposed the undeviating commitment of the communist leaders to the Soviet leadership and their acceptance of the proposition that membership in the communist community in itself best served the national interests of the member states. The latter assumption proved to be a fatal error, for in the new situation the communist leaders fell victim to the pressures and ambitions that confront the leaders of any national complex.

In the archetypal Stalinist situation the alternatives for the Communist parties were clear. A Communist was one who adhered to Stalinist internationalism. Deviationists were forced out of the movement, deprived by definition of their right to be called communist. They became Trotskyists, independent Marxists, a-politicals, or what have you, but not leaders or participants in significant, independent communist movements. This was due partly to the compulsion of old loyalties which deterred them from undertaking organized and militant action against the established international, and partly to the fact that deviationists have no secure power base of their own to attract dissatisfied party members.

In the new postwar situation, however, various alternatives were opened to the national communist parties. They could try to break completely with the Soviet Union and communism, as was finally attempted in Hungary. They could opt for complete internal independence, but render unconditional support to Soviet foreign policy (Poland). They could establish a completely independent communist state, professing to follow their own inclinations in both domestic and foreign policy (Yugoslavia and China). As a general pattern, there was a tendency to establish mastery in their respective houses to the extent that they thought they could avoid penalty at the hands of Soviet military force. The behavior of the communist states began to approximate that of any small country which has to gear both its domestic and external policies to the wishes of the dominant power of the area. The parallel may be strained, but, considering the brief period the communist states have been in existence compared to other states with a time-worn pattern of formulating domestic and foreign policies with an eye to placating the neighboring or dominant big power, the tendency of the former toward the effective exercise of sovereignty has been remarkable.

Objective conditions for the establishment of independent communist states existed at the end of World War Two or even earlier. Tito, for example, had at his command a loyal apparatus and army and considerable popular following, and he probably could have counted on Western support. Tito, however, had no desire to make the break. His views and internal policies were more orthodox than the Pope's. What impelled him to take the step to independence was Stalin's intention to reduce him, through various devices, to the status of a puppet, perhaps worse. Thus the decision was made in the face of the overriding commitment to internationalism and the Soviet Union. His revolt was successful precisely because it took the form of a nationalist revolt against Soviet hegemony, and also because, as is sometimes overlooked, Stalin did not exercise the option of sending troops into Yugoslavia. Stalin exerted various forms of pressure on Tito—internal subversion by "Cominform Communists," economic pressure, border provocations, and so forth—but he did not send in troops. Stalin's behavior is interesting in the light of Khrushchev's later performances in Poland and Hungary and invites speculation on the Kremlin's willingness or unwillingness to take risks. Was Stalin's failure to employ troops the result of a miscalculation? Did he really think he could cause Tito's fall by "shaking his finger"? This seems a reasonable supposition in the light of communist history under Stalin. Nevertheless, at some point Stalin must have recognized that Tito would get away with it unless troops were employed. Did Stalin perhaps calculate that he could not fight Tito to a successful conclusion? Or was the risk perhaps not worth taking at a time of intense US–USSR conflict in Europe? Was it the fear of American intervention to protect the independence of Yugoslavia that deterred him? We do not know.[3] What is apparent, however, was the attraction of national power even to the trained international *apparatchik*, the support for revolt against Moscow not only by non-communists but by most of the communist cadres, and the feasibility of capitalizing on international tensions to achieve independence, at least in certain circumstances.

The Yugoslav break created a potential second center in the communist movement. That it attracted only scattered support is due to a number of factors. In the first place, there was a psychological barrier to condoning a revolt from Moscow. It could not happen and, if it did, it could not be successful. The Yugoslav performance violated all standards of communist behavior. Second, Yugoslav communism at the time—it was to make up for this later—had no distinctive ideas to offer other Communists around which they could rally if they were so minded. Having asserted Yugoslavia's independence, Tito could not even proclaim the virtues of national independence since this violated his ingrained idea of communist internationalism and devotion to the Soviet Union. Third, the leaders of the Eastern European communist parties did not consciously wish to break with Moscow. Their positions depended on the Soviet force behind them; they had no indigenous support. The act of will—not merely the objective circumstances—figures decisively in the circumstances of revolt.

The objective situation which favored the Yugoslav bid for independence existed also in Albania and China. The communist parties in these countries had come to power largely through their own efforts; their geographical position militated against a Soviet attack; and the leaders of the parties were not Moscow men in the same sense that the leaders in the Eastern European countries were. Yet they supported the Soviet Union at that time for motives of their own. The Albanian position, then as now, was a function of its relation with Yugoslavia. The Albanian communist leadership joined in the Cominform attack for the purpose of freeing itself from the Yugoslav tutelage that had been imposed during the war. The Chinese Communists were too preoccupied with the seizure of power to concern themselves with European communist politics. As a result, Albanian and Chinese support of Moscow made them appear to be as tightly bound to Moscow as the other parties. Although certain Western analysts conceded that in principle geographical factors gave the Albanian and Chinese Communists an option denied to the Eastern European communist parties, it was argued that the economic dependence of the latter on the Soviet Union, if no other reason, would preserve their allegiance. The Tito defection, instead of calling attention to the possibilities of revolt, paradoxically served to strengthen belief in the monolithic nature of the communist movement. In particular, it tended to obscure the independence of the Chinese communist regime, since the Chinese Communists, on the establishment of their state, professed their loyalty to Moscow.

In itself, the Yugoslav case testified to the breakdown of Soviet authority in the communist movement and the inadequacy of prewar Soviet institutions to cope with the situation. Stalin's response, nevertheless, was to carry on as usual, or more so, following Tito's defection, by employing purge, terror, and intimidation in Eastern Europe to insure the loyalty of the communist leaders and cadres. Yet this Stalinist method of rule, extended through the leadership of the communist countries, proved to be counterproductive. The ruling hierarchies became increasingly alienated from the people; economic dislocation, particularly in agriculture, continued; living standards did not markedly improve; popular discontent grew. Nevertheless, restructuring of the movement had to await Khrushchev's forceful, if ambiguous, moves at the time of the Twentieth CPSU Congress in February 1956. These served, however, to channel the latent divisive forces in directions unforeseen by Khrushchev.

DE-STALINIZATION AND INTERNATIONAL
FRAGMENTATION

External communist affairs had for years been a function of Soviet policy concerns; the pattern in 1956 was no different. Khrushchev's gambit at the Twentieth Congress was to attempt to consolidate his power and win public backing by dramatically breaking with the past in the person and practice of Stalin.

Yet this denigration of Stalin automatically weakened the authority of the Soviet Union. For in condemning Stalin's method of operation and his brutal treatment of Communists, and virtually accusing him of paranoia, Khrushchev was implicitly condemning the type of relation that had existed between the Soviet Union and the individual communist parties. To rectify the situation, Khrushchev proposed to corporealize the principle that relations between communist states should be based on equality and national self-determination in the construction of socialism. (Reference to the equality of parties as a formalism had been abundant in Stalinist literature.) This was forecast in the Belgrade Declaration of 1955, climaxing Khrushchev's visit to Yugoslavia for the purpose of wooing Tito back to the fold. The idea of equality between parties was reinforced at the Twentieth Congress by Khrushchev's prescription of national and multiple roads to socialism, including the thesis that the nonruling communist parties could achieve power by a variety of means, peaceful or violent, though the accent was placed on peaceful and parliamentary takeover. In the wake of the Polish riots and the Hungarian uprising in 1956, the Soviet leadership issued a further "Declaration" on intercommunist relations:

United by the common ideals of building a socialist society and by the principles of proletarian internationalism, the countries of the great commonwealth of socialist nations can build their mutual relations only on the principles of complete equality, of respect for territorial integrity, state independence and sovereignty, and of non-interference in one another's internal affairs.[4]

National sovereignty and proletarian internationalism are, however, incompatible on many levels of
action. Internationalism, the appeal to unity stemming
from Marxism-Leninism, was meaningless so long as
the parties did not agree on what Marxism-Leninism
prescribed, either for the international scene or more
particularly for their domestic policies. This is a point,
apparently, that the Soviet Communists simply refused, and still refuse, to recognize, for the very good
reason that if they did, a substantial part of their argument for primacy, openly or tacitly held, would be
lost. Moreover, it was not clear at that time whether
the equality Khrushchev spoke about in reference to
the Yugoslavs was the same sort of equality he had
in mind for the other communist parties. With the
Yugoslavs he had no choice but to concede it as a
preliminary to the attempt to heal the breach in the
communist movement and to associate Yugoslavia more
closely with the Soviet Union. In the case of the other
parties, it seems more likely that all Khrushchev had
in mind—even that a considerable step forward—was
to clear the atmosphere and create a new environment
for the communist movement in which the ruling
parties could improve economic conditions and public
morale and the nonruling parties operate more flexibly within the over-all strategy of peaceful coexistence. Yet Soviet leadership was to be unimpaired, and
the behavior patterns to remain essentially unchanged.
Events, however, served to shape the contours of the
doctrine of equality in a way Khrushchev probably did
not anticipate.

The revolts in Poland and Hungary in 1956, stemming in part from the disintegration of authority
sparked by Khrushchev, seemed to vitiate the new

principles on the basis of which communist relations were to be newly ordered. The flaw in de-Stalinization had become manifest. The decision to downgrade the police, to place intercommunist relations on a more flexible basis, and to afford the local rulers more autonomy in coping with their domestic problems automatically cut into Soviet authority in the international movement. Relaxation brought to the surface popular resentment against the local regimes and against Soviet domination as well. The centrifugal forces were encouraged by the instability of the Soviet regime itself, apparently still fighting out the succession problem. Gomulka's return to power in October 1956, and the forcible suppression of the Hungarian revolt of October–November 1956, damaged Soviet prestige and the cohesion of the communist "bloc" still further.

Unity was temporarily re-established at the November 1957 meeting of the communist parties, which issued a "Declaration" of principles signed by twelve communist parties, Yugoslavia abstaining.[5] The Declaration, to which all parties subsequently adhered, prescribed nine basic "laws" governing all parties engaged in socialist construction. As Khrushchev put it at the Twenty-first CPSU Congress in January 1959, the Declaration was a "charter of international unity for the world communist movement." The advisability of establishing a new international organization was discussed, but nothing came of this. Instead, in what appears to have been a compromise proposal, a decision was made to establish a new international organ to replace the defunct Cominform journal. Entitled *Problems of Peace and Socialism* (the English title is *World Marxist Review: Problems of Peace and Social-*

ism) and published in Prague, it was conceived not as a policy-dispensing journal but rather as a journal of discussion. A further step to promote unity in the absence of a central organization or centralizing conference was the decision to coordinate policy through bilateral and multilateral contacts, of which the most notable example was the convocation of seventeen West European communist parties in Rome in November 1959, under Italian communist auspices.[6]

Although the principle of equality of parties was restated in the Declaration, the operative factor at the November 1957 conference was panic in the movement attributable to "revisionism"—that is, the attempt to overthrow Soviet-oriented communist leaderships. The price of unity was, once again, the alienation of Yugoslavia, which refused to join the other states in signing the Declaration, although it did adhere to a propagandist peace manifesto. From the standpoint of restructuring authority to conform to new conditions, the meeting had accomplished nothing. The problem of how to reconcile Soviet authority with local autonomy and diversity remained. The dilemma was unwittingly underscored by the Soviet theoreticians in their effort to bring the concept of proletarian internationalism up to date in the Soviet textbook, *Osnovy Marksizma-Leninizma* (*Fundamentals of Marxism-Leninism*), which first appeared in 1959. Here proletarian internationalism was defined as

. . . *the scientifically confirmed ideology of the community of interests of the working classes of all countries and nations. Secondly, it is the feeling of solidarity of the working people of all countries. . . . Thirdly, it is a definite form taken by the relations between the national detachments of the working class. These relations are based on unity and concerted action, mutual aid .and support. The special characteristic of these relations is that they are built on a voluntary basis. . . .*

Proletarian internationalism in no way denies the independence of the different national detachments of the working class or their right to make their own decisions. However, this does not at all impair the unity of the international working class. On the contrary, precisely because a spirit of true equality and respect for the interests of the workers of different nations reigns in the politically conscious international working-class movement, mutual confidence and striving for cooperation become ever more deeply rooted among the working people of all countries.[7]

The leading role of the Soviet Union, explicit in Stalin's version of proletarian internationalism, is still there but more weakly and indirectly stated. The Soviet Union is still designated the "vanguard and bulwark" of the international movement, and its experience has "international significance" but ". . . being the vanguard and bulwark does not, of course, in any way mean interfering in the internal affairs of other states and 'making' resolutions there."[8] Thus, the Declaration of 1957 proclaimed communist cohesion under Soviet control and the theoreticians wrote it down, but the decentralizing tendencies persisted and were accelerated by the Chinese Communists who, after playing a unifying role in 1957, administered a *coup de grâce* in 1960 to the tradition of unchallenged Soviet leadership in the international communist movement.

THE CONTEST FOR LEADERSHIP

The Sino-Soviet showdown took place at the conference of the eighty-one communist parties in Moscow, November 1960, at which the Soviet leaders attempted to re-establish their discipline over the Chinese—and over the movement. They sought to establish the principle of majority rule—that decisions once made should be binding on all parties and factionalism should be condemned. They also sought to reaffirm their leading role in the international movement—despite Khrushchev's disavowal of the title "leader of the camp"—by asking the conference to endorse the decisions of the Twentieth and Twenty-first party Congresses—that is, endorse the general Soviet line in international relations, de-Stalinization, and other areas.

The Russians took a decisive beating on all counts. The Chinese reiterated their proposition that complete equality must obtain between parties, arguing that criticism is not incompatible with unity. Moreover, they declared that the concept of equality implied that there were no superior or subordinate parties and therefore it was not seemly to demand that one party submit to another. Subordination to the majority along the lines of democratic centralism, the Chinese averred, was a principle that applied to the internal relations of individual parties, not to interparty relations. They also denied the general applicability of the Twentieth and Twenty-first Congresses to the international movement, stating that what was correct in these two Congresses, let alone their errors, did not apply to other parties. What came out of the conference was a statement of banalities which thinly concealed the failure of Khrushchev to impose discipline on the movement—to impose his own version of proletarian internationalism, based on majority rule, for Stalin's version. Khrushchev's resort to the majority principle was in itself a sign of the erosion of Soviet authority. His failure to have that principle accepted formally marks the beginning of the polycentric phase of world communism. A diffusion of power was generated in the communist movement, making it more nearly a political movement with a mutuality of give and take than it had been since the twenties. The positions of the national communist parties have been strengthened in the process, with Moscow and China soliciting their support.

The People's Republic of China, from its creation in 1949, has occupied a special status within the international communist movement. An independent center of power, it had nevertheless acceded to Moscow's leading role in the movement and moreover has been one of the staunchest advocates of communist unity. Its role as a sort of silent, supporting junior partner was doubtless determined in its early years by the need to consolidate its power and to receive economic and technical aid from the communist world and in external affairs to avail itself of Moscow's support against Chiang Kai-shek and the United States. Nevertheless, its influence within the communist orbit had grown, particularly in Asia, through its participation in the Korean War, its geographical position in relation to North Vietnam, and its increased presence in Outer Mongolia after the Sino-Soviet agreements of October

1954. China's domestic problems, furthermore, have inspired solutions (such as the communes in 1948), which actually produced a sympathetic response from the Bulgarian, Czech, East German, and North Korean regimes, even though they departed from Soviet practice; and its foreign policies, particularly its relations —or nonrelations—with the United States, have promoted an attitude toward external affairs different from the Russian. These latent divisive factors were supplemented by China's critical reception of the Twentieth CPSU Congress and de-Stalinization,[9] which set the stage for the later open challenge to Soviet authority. But the Chinese leap into prominence was, paradoxically, as peacemaker in communist Europe. The Chinese supported the Polish Communists in their bid for independent status and urged Soviet use of force to put down the Hungarian revolt. But most dramatic was Premier Chou En-lai's interruption of an Asian tour in order to visit Moscow, Warsaw, and Budapest and pledge Chinese support to a unified bloc under Soviet leadership.[10] China had emerged as a power in communist affairs as a whole and by coming to the aid of the Soviet Union had called attention to the erosion of Moscow's authority and correspondingly to its own prominent role in international communist affairs.

It is not my purpose to review the history of the Sino-Soviet dispute; in general the events and issues have been recorded, and the outpourings of the protagonists themselves have made kremlinology in this aspect of communist affairs obsolete. The polemic, involving the exchange of hundreds of thousands of words, has been conducted around the central issues of war and peace, transitional forms to socialism, and relations with the non-communist world, particularly with the United States. These issues, argued in ideological terms, have reflected differences with regard to internal and external policy and, more deeply, to the Soviet Union's very attitude toward the People's Republic of China, to which it apparently would not intrust nuclear weapons. Essentially, the polemic involved the question: who was to determine policy— that is, the question of authority in the communist movement.

The Chinese challenge to constituted authority is traditional in form but entirely new in content. Like previous Communists who have constituted factions within particular parties or within the communist movement as a whole, the Chinese are attempting to persuade other Communists to change the policies and direction of the movement. They suggest that, like Lenin in his fight within the Russian Social Democratic Party, they are merely a temporary minority which will soon be converted into a majority. In fact, it should be stressed that the Chinese have carried on their fight *within* the movement, and the particular nationalistic policies which have contributed to the Sino-Soviet rift are meshed with their prescriptions for the communist movement as a whole. In conducting their polemic, they employ a rule of thumb which differs little from that of Stalin, the operating principle being that what was good for the Soviet Union was good for all communist parties.

If the form of the challenge is traditional, nevertheless the situational aspect is novel. The Chinese challenge was not aimed at freeing the Chinese from

Moscow; they were already free and independent. Its purpose was rather to purge the communist movement of Moscow-oriented policies in favor of policies acceptable to the Chinese. In other words, the Chinese, at an earlier stage at least, hoped to continue to have the USSR as their shield and supplier. In such an arrangement lay their greatest strength. Chinese insistence that the Soviet Union be recognized as the leader of the camp was thus no empty rhetoric. But the insistence that the Soviet Union alter its international policies to conform more nearly with Chinese views meant, in effect, a demand for joint Sino-Soviet leadership of the communist movement, an arrangement that seems to have occurred to Molotov in 1955.[11] Authority in the communist movement—though the Chinese never made themselves explicit on this point—was to be vested in a condominium. But how can rule be shared in a political system made up of diverging national interests that has been accustomed to one leader and one authoritative spokesman?

The failure of the Chinese Communists to bring around their Russian erstwhile colleagues resulted in open rivalry for leadership in the communist movement with the resultant realignment of parties, formation of pro-Chinese splinter parties, and creation of factions within the several communist parties. The conditions of battle have provided the parties opportunity to improve their own positions within the movement, accelerating the tendency toward the independence Khrushchev postulated. In China the Albanians found a cover for their defiance of Moscow, whose rerapprochement with Yugoslavia had become too comfortable for suspicious Albanian sensibilities. Moscow's need to retain supporters makes it easier for other parties to put forward their own interests, as Rumania did in connection with the Council on Mutual Economic Assistance (Comecon). The Communist Party of New Zealand, which does not have a ghost of a chance of seizing power but which nevertheless wishes to act as if it did, capitalized on the rift by choosing to follow the more traditional communist orientation of Communist China. The rift has smoked out the die-hard Stalinists who, in trouble after Khrushchev's campaign against Stalinism, have been able to assert themselves in alignment with Peking.

The momentum toward independence has also been expressed in terms of regional preferences. In the advanced countries of the West, where revolution is not on the order of the day, sympathy with Khrushchev's policies has, with exceptions, preserved the traditional orientation to Moscow. Even as monolithic a party as the French under that hard-bitten Stalinist, the late Maurice Thorez, joined the anti-Chinese forces because it knew that its destiny (whatever that may be) was bound up with European Russia, not with an Asian power. Conversely, the Asian communist parties have with few exceptions tended to support Communist China. Ho Chi Minh, the leader of a communist party in a country traditionally unfriendly to China and, moreover, an astute politician who has attempted to maximize his independence and avoid taking sides in the controversy, has for reasons of geography and logistics leaned to the side of the Chinese.

In sum, postwar nationalism has infected the communist movement, eroding its vaunted internationalism. If the particular concatenation of events had not taken place, one might speculate that nationalist forces might yet have asserted themselves. As it is, the battle is being fought out by the autonomists versus the Stalinists, the reformists versus the traditionalists, and the pragmatists versus the doctrinaires. On another level, the battle is being joined to preserve the communist movement as an international force and, in so doing, it is feeding nationalist tendencies and the impulse toward greater autonomy and independence. The development is complex; there are ninety communist parties of differing size and influence, functioning in a variety of conditions with widely varying prospects, and their motives and objectives consequently vary widely. Can a pattern of behavior be discerned on closer examination of the individual communist parties?

4. THE EXISTING ALTERNATIVES

Much of the writing on the postwar communist movement was influenced by a model of communism distinguished by its totalitarian, ideological determinist, and monolithic features. Such a construct, reflecting at least a part of the existing reality, was suggestive, even though it slighted the symptomatic and the historical. Generally ignored was behavior that deviated from the totalitarian model, together with factors which normally affect the world's politics—for example national differences and the impulse toward the exercise of sovereignty. The favored—"totalitarian"—approach, at least in the United States, was reinforced by the kind of social pressure and hysteria in the support of American foreign policy which was symbolized by McCarthyism.

When the myth of communist unity was exploded by the Chinese Communists' open challenge to Soviet hegemony in the sixties, nationalism and national communism became the preoccupations of analysts of communist affairs. This was natural and necessary, but it risked neglect of certain factors that still tended to promote cohesion in the communist movement. Nationalist sentiment affecting the communist movement was seen as part of the general eruption of nationalist forces after World War Two, whether such forces were achieving the independence of the former colonial countries or asserting sovereignty in Western Europe. No doubt there is something to this view, but the quality and circumstances of the nationalisms are too disparate for comfortable generalization. The nationalism in Africa, for example, is partly a generative one, an attempt to create a national consciousness for national sovereignties, many of which are artificially created. This nationalism, an automatic concomitant of European withdrawal, is but the prelude, it may be imagined, to amalgamation, African imperialism, and integration. Western European nationalism circa 1960 bears little relationship to African nationalism, and its content is different from that of nineteenth-century European nationalism. Western European nationalism is the product of the successful postwar rehabilitation, the resurgence of national pride, and discontent with American tutelage. It is exemplified by that grand anachronism, Charles de Gaulle. Yet this expression of nationalism takes place against a counter development, and perhaps in the long run a more important one—that is, the institutionalization of European cooperation. Communist nationalism is something else again. For whereas communist states reflect some parallels in the assertion of economic and political sovereignty and certain communist parties exhibit a trend toward independent expression and autonomy, the modalities of the movement are quite different and exercise their own constraints.

The international communist movement in 1965 numbered about ninety communist parties with a membership of from 44 million to 45 million.[1] These figures reflect a lesser reality. Ninety per cent of the world membership is concentrated in the fourteen communist states, including Cuba and Yugoslavia. A large part of this membership is purely nominal. Similarly, roughly three-quarters of the membership of the non-ruling communist parties is accounted for by that of the Indonesian and Italian parties. Approximately forty of the parties are proscribed or operate under restrictive conditions. Certain of the parties are represented in the national legislatures. Many of them merely exist on paper. A large proportion of them are negligible as political forces. In the communist "bloc," curiously enough, despite the existence of international organizations for regulating broadcasting and river and railroad traffic, there had been little effort under Stalin and even under his successors to set up intergovernmental organizations that would provide a measure of institutional control. The possibility of "decomposition" was therefore all the greater. In short, the heterogeneity of the parties, in terms of size, influence, social composition, *modus operandi*, potential for seizure of power, or, in the case of the ruling parties, the effectiveness of political socialization, defies attempts at generalization. If this was true in the Stalinist period—the heterogeneity was particularly a feature of the movement in the decade after World War Two—how much more difficult it is in the present period of dissension and fission to generalize on trends and alignments. Various writers, including this one, have attempted to trace trends in the communist movement by constructing a spectrum or continuum of political orientation, showing, for example, which parties supported Moscow on its ostracism of Albania at different times, or reflecting the support or nonsupport of Moscow on ideological versus organizational matters and the like. Such efforts at analysis are enjoyable exercises for the writers (or at least for this one), and many were instructive, if inconclusive. The parties, or at least some of them—the qualification immediately pinpoints the problem—are behaving more independently than was their custom. How, first, can their differentiated behavior be explained? What are their motives? What are their goals? To attempt an answer to these questions, the traditional approach to analysis of the communist movement must be revised.

THE REVERSED OPTION

Trends in the communist movement were, in the past, generally discerned by focusing on the policies of the center—of Moscow—and then scrutinizing the adjustments made by the national communist parties. The more sophisticated analysis paid closer attention to the national parties in order to observe the interaction between the national party and the center, aware that at times there was an interplay of pressures and less than optimum compliance. But the rule of thumb held; motivation and line came from the top down. With the breakdown of authority in the international communist movement, however, the direction is seemingly reversed. The national parties have the option; the burden is on them. It is not that simple, of course, but the point is worth emphasis if only to throw a new perspective on communist behavior. In principle nothing prevents the national parties from continuing the closest relationship with Moscow. By the same token, nothing prevents them from transferring the same type of relationship to Peking. Alternatively, nothing prevents any of them from asserting its independence and functioning as an indigenous communist party, even taking a new name, within its own countries.

The point has now been overstated. The choice of action of the individual communist party, like that of the non-communist party, is circumscribed by tradition and environment.

More than any other political party, the communist party can be said to have existed more for others than for itself. The idea of the perfectibility of man through an international society of justice was its origin. "The International shall be the human race." International solidarity was its organizational principle. However perverted the internationalism became in the service of the Soviet state, internationalism remained as a reason for being. Take away the internationalism and what remains? A number of so-called communist parties structured more or less similarly, depending on the area, and professing more or less radical principles, again depending on the area. Deprived of their international links, the parties would be fated to compromise with the environment to maintain and increase power, and though they might be successful, would they remain communist? In other words, it is internationalism itself, however transfigured, that has been the crucial bond of the communist movement. Stalin, once described by his followers as a "political genius," a title which history may yet confer upon him, recognized the importance of internationalism as a binding force when he admonished the Communists to guard unity as the "apple of their eye." Moscow fears the loss in its quarrel with Peking. Peking accuses Moscow of having sacrificed internationalism to nationalism. The national communist Tito hovers in the wings attempting to rejoin the internationalist forces—in an acceptable arrangement, of course. Castro knows the value of internationalism: he became an ex-post-facto Marxist-Leninist to obtain the support necessary to sustain his independence from the United States. Trotsky was substantially correct in his view that national revolution would be successful only under the protective covering of revolution on an international scale. For comfort in time of trial and encouragement in moments of revolutionary offensive, the national parties drew sustenance from their links with the international movement.

Nevertheless, the incontrovertible effect of the Sino-Soviet dispute has been a centrifugal development in the international communist movement, dramatized by such acts of independence as the refusal of several communist parties to fall in with Soviet plans at the end of 1964 to convoke a world-wide meeting for the presumed purpose of excommunicating the Chinese Communists. Interestingly enough, however, amid the accumulated evidence of independent action on the part of many parties, there have been few statements defining with any clarity the concept of the new autonomy or independence. After forty-five years of varying association in a movement which stressed its internationalism, a reluctance to go much beyond affirming that the parties are independent is understandable. The reluctance may not be caused by considerations of a public-relations nature or by the consideration that inadequate time has elapsed to articulate the new concepts of polycentrism or independence or autonomy. Rather it may simply result from the fact that a large number of parties do not favor the scrapping of an international orientation for a national one. The prospect of national independence in a movement that merely pays lip service to internationalism may be distasteful, if not frightening. The weaker parties, fearing isolation and government and Western pressures, find a measure of security in subservience to the Soviet Union, which perpetuates cultivated patterns of behavior and assures them of support. Weakness and fear tend to reinforce ideological conviction and the stake in the *status quo.* Subservience to the Soviet Union is not automatically a liability. Even those parties which feel up to the task of independent decision-making may wish to preserve the movement not merely as *pro forma* internationalism but as internationalism which does maintain a coherent orientation and which sets general policy goals within whose framework the local parties decide their own strategies and tactics to their best advantage. Yet such an arrangement, which may appear plausible in the writing, is not so easily accomplished. Exhortations for solidarity and unity are no substitute for institutionalization of arrangements to resolve conflicts.

THE ITALIAN PARTY AND AUTONOMY

Of the parties which have most strongly stressed autonomy and independent decision-making, the Italian has been the most articulate in commenting on new forms of interparty relations. In the discussions that took place after the posthumous publication of Togliatti's Yalta memorandum[2] of August 1964, which opposed, among others, the proposals to reconstitute a centralized international organization, the Italian Communist Party leaders made it clear that they wished to break neither with communism as an international phenomenon nor with the idea that the national parties should function within the framework of a general policy. As put by one of its leaders, Enrico Berlinguer, the Italian party ". . . in no way wants to stand aside, on the outside looking in, but . . . intends firmly to remain within the camp of the CP's and within the framework of their solidarity and collaboration."[3] To Togliatti was ascribed the ". . . vision which tended to place the party issues and the problems within the communist movement in a broader framework, a framework which always takes as its point of departure the general interests of the working classes and the consciousness of the decisive responsibilities which the communist movement has assumed for the sake of the destiny and future of all mankind."[4] The eschatological vision is reaffirmed.

If the parties are still to be bound in proletarian internationalism as redefined, what are the parameters of their latitude as indigenous parties? Here the Italians make a distinction between independence and autonomy. Independence (*indipendenza*) is not at issue. The party claims to be fully independent. What is at issue is "autonomy" (*autonomia*). Independence presupposes autonomy, but autonomy is still something less than independence in the sense in which the Republican Party in the United States would think of itself as independent. This is undoubtedly a confusing and perhaps unworkable proposition. The textual formulation may be of help: Autonomy, it is asserted, is

the only valid road, the irreplaceable means through which we can assure the political development of each and every party. This development, as a matter of fact, can come about only when we proceed from an adherence, from general statements, and from propaganda to an objective analysis of the specific realities of each country, and, on the basis of this, to a precise determination of the objectives and forms of the struggle which are bound to differ from one country to the next, as well as to initiative and daily political action. However, contained within autonomy understood and practiced in this manner, we also have the basis for unity and we are talking here about a healthier and more substantial unity for the entire movement.[5]

Autonomy, as the Italians use it, defines the functional relationship between the individual party and the communist parties considered as an international movement. The former guiding center which prescribed the norms of internationalism has been merged into internationalism itself. In the context of Stalin-style proletarian internationalism, authority was lodged in the center. Policy was handed down from the top and the individual parties adjusted to it. In the context of what we may call autonomous internationalism (reminiscent of Trotsky's "reciprocal relations"—see page 30), authority is lodged in the consensus of the individual parties. A general—international—orientation is derived from the agreement worked out by the several parties but the implementation of the general line will follow the dictates of the individual parties. Autonomy implies not only the right of each party to work out its policy for itself but also the right to make its contribution to the general strategy. This Italian proposition furthermore implies the development of conscious and substantial autonomy in all communist parties to prevent the atomization and isolation which threatens the parties as a result of the disintegration of Moscow as a central directing agency and the fragmentation of the communist movement. The argument seems to be that if each party is fully alert to its own peculiar problems and is confident in articulating and defending them, the communist movement as a whole will be revitalized and able to function as a unity despite the multifarious situations confronting the parties. This is what is apparently meant by the formula, "Unity amid difference, unity amid autonomy."[6]

CONFLICT BETWEEN AUTONOMY AND UNITY

But there are problems. The Italian concept of the autonomous international has no room for an international organization with executive power or for a command party.[7] Decisions governing the general line or common goals of the international communist movement would therefore have to be taken by common consent. Agreement on a general line cannot easily be achieved by ninety parties which, as a matter of record, view the world and the problems of the international movement in strikingly different ways. Decision by majority rule does not seem to be a feasible mechanism. The Chinese, for example, conceding that majority rule is an appropriate method for regulating intraparty affairs, have nevertheless rejected it for interparty relations. Again, in the debate surrounding the international meeting which the Russians attempted to convoke in 1964-1965, one of the stumbling blocks was the principle of majority rule, because of the likelihood that the CPSU, which probably could have commanded the support of a majority of the parties, would have been in a position to impose its will on recalcitrant parties. In the Italian formula as well, then, forcing the minority to accept majority decisions would be a violation of party autonomy. In the present stage of strife in the communist movement, there are thus two obstacles to majority rule as the organizing principle of the international movement: the ability of the CPSU to command a majority, and, more subtly, sabotage of the majority principle to play for time to permit the communist parties to enlarge the area of autonomy which might be denied them if they submitted to majority rule at this time.

If majority rule is out, decision by consensual agreement seems to be an even more remote possibility, except on broad, essentially meaningless propaganda statements. Consensual agreement implies at least a shared world outlook, which the Sino-Soviet conflict, all quotations from Marx and Lenin by Communists and non-Communists to the contrary notwithstanding, has demonstrated does not exist. Communist assertion of the eventual triumph of communism over capitalism matters less than awareness of how remote the possibility is in many areas and, more pertinently, unwillingness to jeopardize tangible interests for nebulous prospects.

Perhaps the greatest obstacles to the development of an autonomous international is the apparent reluctance of many parties to accept an autonomous status. This is a curious assertion and one, moreover, that is not backed up by much evidence. Negative support for this proposition is the absence of impressive discussion of the subject within the parties, coupled with their performance along old lines. Old patterns of behavior are difficult to break. A suggestion that the assertion is not, however, without foundation emanates again from the Italian party, which referred to autonomy ". . . in its most substantial and profound meaning as a stimulus for search and discussion, a stimulus for creative development and for the political growth of every party."[8] The statement implies that the parties by and large remain in a stultified state and that, for the movement to develop new resources, each party must begin to grapple with its own problems and work out its own ideas. Otherwise the present fluid situation, which offers the opportunity for autonomous development, will be lost. The reluctance of weak parties to do more than go through the motions of working out indigenous programs and strategies in areas where the objective situation gives them little encouragement is understandable.

Viewing the development of an autonomous international from another angle, it is difficult to comprehend how the flowering of autonomy will promote unity. The very objective of breaking old patterns to achieve a substantial autonomy can only serve to accelerate the centrifugal tendencies in the movement. The argument for autonomy urges that confidence in one's party will establish a tolerance for cooperation at an international level. In principle this sounds good. But the assertion that diversity can exist in unity has all the earmarks of a dialectic that is plausible on paper but impossible in practice—if unity is meant to be anything more than *pro forma* internationalism.[9] The divergent interests of the parties are such that, everything else being equal (for example, the absence of international crisis which would tend to bring the communist parties together), the substance of unity could take only the most clichéd forms. And even this may be saying too much, for though everyone is for peace, the peace that is desired differs now even among the communist parties.

The unity-autonomy syndrome has another dimension that threatens not only the factor of unity but the character of the communist parties as well. The question arises whether a polycentric (nonmonolithic) system can be reconciled with the existence of monolithic (command-type) communist parties. Polycentrism calls for toleration of diversity and a more permissive and decentralized arrangement among communist parties. Would not similar pressures for toleration and permissiveness be operative within the communist parties themselves? If there is a correlation between loosening up on interparty and on intraparty levels, what assurance is there that unity can be maintained on either the national or international level? Is it the beginning of the end for national as well as for international communism?

Apart from the subjective aspects of the problem— that is, the intentions and designs of the various parties —there remain the objective factors limiting the possibility of development of truly independent national parties bound together in a cohesive international. In the advanced capitalist countries, not one of the parties in Europe, North America, or the British Commonwealth has the remotest chance of seizing power. Only three—the French, Italian, and Finnish—are political factors of any consequence in their respective countries. However flawed the structure of welfare capitalism, revolution as a consequence of the crisis of capitalism in the Marxian sense is not a serious possibility. Revolution as a consequence of crisis provoked by war can also safely be excluded, since a war in Europe would take on the character of a world war whose outcome would be determined by the US and the USSR and not by the action of the local communist parties—if there were anything left to be determined. Communist parties as classic revolutionary parties are therefore anachronisms in the Western world. Is there a possibility that in changed circumstances the character of the revolution has also changed and the parties have as their goal the achievement of peaceful revolution? The perspectives of the Twentieth CPSU Congress suggest the possibility of peaceful and parliamentary transition to power, and the communist parties have incorporated this slogan into their programs. Again, excluding the resistance to a takeover that would be offered by the traditional forces,′ with or without American collaboration, only the three parties previously mentioned have the possibility of translating this approach into successful politics. But more crucial to the nature of the problem is the fact that in order to win the support necessary to achieve a parliamentary majority, the parties labor under the necessity of making themselves and their programs palatable to the electorate. They must be indigenous; they must be open; they must be limited in their objectives because, except to radical intellectuals and the disaffected artistic and the "beats," welfare capitalism has satisfied—or is in the process of satisfying—the wants and desires of the people. If questions still exist concerning the fashioning of a more rational society, or concerning the problem of alienation as a result of the total structuring of the personality through the prevalent ideology and mass communications, or the like, they are not the questions of the masses, or even of the mainstream of intellectuals. For a communist party to exist as an effective political force, it must take on the coloration of the bourgeois parties, whether they are called Labour, Conservative, Christian Democrat, or simply Democratic.

A standard rebuttal to this line of argument is that whatever the Communists would do in this respect is tactical. Having achieved power through constitutional means, they would then unmask their true aims and communize the country. But the chameleon act is not quite so simple for a political party. As has already been pointed out, most of the parties in the Western world do not have the potential to seize power by either peaceful or violent means. Those few that do have the theoretical possibility would have to alter themselves radically to gain the support needed to achieve the margin of victory. And even if they did eventually still show their communist hand, what would that mean in real terms, in terms of the organization of the economy, social structure, and the like? Developments in Eastern Europe have shown that nationalization of industry is no open sesame—nor are the majority of citizens in the East or West vitally affected by such measures. Collectivization of agriculture is a failure; market mechanisms are being restored progressively in the East. What else then? The molding of socialist man? In foreign policy it could mean alliance with the Soviet Union, but even here what was once axiomatic is in doubt in the light of the behavior of certain of the Eastern European countries. The greatest fear, of course, is that once in power, the communist parties will suppress all opposition and establish a terroristic state. The possibility cannot be denied in the face of experience. Yet a transformed party may not necessarily behave according to past patterns which have come under increasing criticism. It may indeed permit itself to be voted out of office.

It seems clear, then, that the alternatives open to the communist parties are strictly limited. They can continue, as they have for almost half a decade, to act as if they were part of an internationalist movement, taking their cues from the center. In doing so, they make their contribution to the fight against world capitalism and imperialism, and that may be reward enough. The acquisition of a greater measure of autonomy, one of the major consequences of the Sino-Soviet rift, does not help them very much. For what is the autonomy to be used? To direct an indigenous revolutionary movement for which the objective conditions are totally lacking? The parties can utilize their autonomy to translate the international line more intelligently into local strategy and tactics. Such a course may preserve them from repression and political disasters but does not offer much in the way of overcoming their present minority status in their respective countries. Autonomy may also allow them to support certain measures of their countries' foreign policy which once would have seemed unorthodox, but such action would tend to identify them with the other political parties. For most of the communist parties in the advanced countries, then, autonomy of policy is a less substantial gain than it appears to be so far as the acquisition of political power is concerned. The conclusion suggests itself that although the behavior of the parties may be freer and they may voice their criticism of Soviet policies as well as of the policies of their respective leaders, the limitations on their power will reinforce their identification with internationalism, even if this in fact means identification with a particular center.

THE LINGERING INTERNATIONAL COMMITMENT

There is one major qualification to this line of analysis which affects not the remarks on autonomy but those on the role of internationalism and the center.

For if it is accurate to say that the essential aspect of the function of the communist parties in the advanced countries is the promotion of the struggle against capitalism in general, the question arises how is this best accomplished. And it is precisely on this point that the Chinese Communists have made their intervention. Their invective against the revisionist policies of the Soviet leadership boils down to an attitude which holds that no matter what the condition of a communist party is, it should behave as one. This means that whatever circumstances exist to limit a communist party in carrying out its policies, it should conduct itself as a revolutionary party, making no bones about its intention to destroy capitalism and imperialism, fight the United States, support the national liberation movements and the radical states established in the underdeveloped areas. It is fundamentalism versus revisionism and struggle versus accommodation.

It is this question of *attitude*, it seems to me, that most nearly explains the adhesion of the Communist Party of New Zealand to the Peking axis and the fractionalization of the Belgian Communist Party instigated by the influential Brussels leadership. That the New Zealand Communist Party of some five hundred members, polling less than one per cent of the vote at the last national election in 1963, should opt for the more revolutionary outlook of Peking, on the face of it seems ludicrous. A cynic might explain the phenomenon as a reaction against the boredom of the welfare state. But it makes sense in terms of the commitment to revolutionary Marxism-Leninism. Without the slightest chance of achieving power, the party behaves as if it has, at the same time throwing its allegiance to the new revolutionary Chinese power whose support to outside revolutionary movements is as yet above suspicion. The examples of the New Zealand Party and the dissident Belgian Communist Party illustrate the alternative open to the Western communist parties which, unable to visualize the seizure of power in their own countries, nevertheless are willing to throw in their lot with revolutionary internationalism. This would appear to be the choice for survival: linkage to internationalism whether revisionist or revolutionary, or disintegration. The full exercise of autonomy which would require the accommodation to and exploitation of local conditions leads down the road to de-communization, except possibly for the French and Italian communist parties. The breakdown of authority in the international communist movement, which provided the preconditions for the development of national authority, does not automatically lead to the exercise of that authority. The new independence has been used to shift alignment from Moscow to Peking, but the shift is still within the framework of internationalism. No nonruling communist party has yet declared its independence of all centers. Of the ruling communist parties which have broken with Moscow, only the Yugoslav is a national communist party, albeit in empathic alliance with Moscow; the others, including the non-ruling groups, are gathered in an internationalist framework centered in Peking, whether as a temporary minority in the world communist movement or as the nucleus of another international. The return to the autonomous relationship existing at the founding of the Comintern is impossible simply because the common outlook which envisaged a series of proletarian national revolts against weakened capitalist regimes culminating in World or European Revolution has long since been dissipated. Western capitalism has grown stronger; communist goals have been transformed or sublimated; conflicts over doctrine and policy are rife in the movement; autonomy is conditioned by the need somehow to preserve the international communist community. Moreover, the exercise of autonomy simply for the sake of the national party was never acceptable even in the heyday of "socialism in one country," let alone now, when turning inward may portend the demise of communist parties as radical alternatives to the existing political parties.

Tradition and need also serve to brake any autonomous tendencies on the part of the communist parties in the underdeveloped areas. Most of them, small in size, negligible in importance, operating under repressive conditions, have no reason for existence except as they are tied to an international movement. Their need for unity was illustrated, for example, in their unwillingness to commit themselves forthrightly to the side of Moscow as the Sino-Soviet dispute developed. With meager internal resources, they have everything to lose in the fragmentation of the international movement, its power and its purpose. A few parties rooted more deeply in the society—the Chilean, for example, 25,000 to 30,000 strong, represented in the national legislature, regarded as a legitimate party, not merely as an alien offshoot of Moscow—could conceivably go their own way; yet they maintain their Soviet lines. Even those parties dissatisfied with the Moscow dispensation show no signs of striking out on their own.

Where dissent is in evidence and the parties have been fractionalized, allegiance has been directed toward Peking. Unlike the situation in the advanced areas where the prospects of achieving power are not on the drafting board, in the underdeveloped areas the fluid nature of politics at least holds out the possibility of successful action. The means commonly employed include semiconspiratorial action and violent methods more in keeping with the Chinese orientation. The communist parties are, moreover, in competition with radical nationalist movements whose methods and ends are not so different from the Communists', presenting both opportunities for collaboration and competition for power. Their method of operation is a more traditional—Leninist—one, and the advice and support of a powerful movement behind them are useful if not indispensable. On the whole, the prospect appears more likely that those parties chafing under Moscow's tutelage will use the present disruption in the communist camp not to strike out on their own but rather to align themselves with Peking or with a powerful regional center if such develops. Castro's Cuba was such a potential center in Latin America, but its development was hampered by Castro's need to cooperate with Moscow's policies, which, so far as Latin America is concerned, require that leadership be left in the hands of the Moscow-oriented parties and that the pursuit of policy not jeopardize Moscow's relations with the United States. A trend toward regionalism, in the form of consultation without permanent organization, established with the meeting of Western European communist parties in Rome in 1959 (see page 63), seems to have been carried forward

with the Brussels conference of the Western European communist parties, held June 1-3, 1965.[10] Yet
regionalism as an alternative to central coordination
and control of policy does not seem to have caught on,
perhaps because it vitiates the essential internationalism of communism and, as a practical matter, raises
the possibility of domination by a single party—the
French or Italian in Western Europe, the Cuban in
Latin America—as well as the possibility of conflict
between leading parties. Regional meetings for purposes of consultation and coordination of strategy
within an international framework are as old as the
Comintern itself, but regionalism as a substitute for
international coordination would, in effect, mean the
end of communism conceived as an international movement.

5. THE POSITION OF
THE RULING PARTIES

The argument, then, is that the nonruling communist parties are independent but that this independence rejects the idea of complete freedom of action. For interrelated reasons of tradition and environment, the parties wish to maintain an internationalist attachment. The problem for many of them is how to strike a balance between their own requirements and an acceptable internationalist orientation without capitulating to the dictation of a dominant center.

The ruling communist parties, for their part, can claim to be independent sovereignties and have shown evidence of it. Yet the question is open as to subjective intentions—that is, to what extent they desire to restrict their dependence on Moscow and limit internationalist constraints. At the same time, it is far from clear what latitude the USSR will permit before it judges that its vital interests are being jeopardized, and also what sanctions are available to it.

EUROPEAN COMMUNIST STATES

The Eastern European and Central European communist parties are considered to be within the Soviet Union's sphere of influence. Influence in these party-states has not been exercised indirectly in the traditional manner of international politics but rather by such direct control as Soviet military occupation and party leaderships hand-picked by the Soviet leaders. Overthrow of the communist governments has been considered to be virtually impossible on the ground that these states exercise total power and, even if a local communist regime could be temporarily overturned, the Soviet Union would restore it by direct intervention. So it appeared, and the sequence of events in the Hungarian revolt is apparent confirmation of this view. Yet it is no longer safe to assume that the Soviet Union will automatically employ or send in its troops to quell a revolt. Most remarkably, in terms of the general conception of Soviet behavior, Stalin did not send in troops to crush Tito. Even more interesting was the unwillingness of the Soviet leaders —if the Chinese Communists can be credited—to dispatch troops the second time to crush the Nagy uprising in Hungary. However, the possibility of non-communist revolt is not at issue here. What is under consideration is the more limited possibility that the communist regimes might expand their sovereignties, making their own decisions in the realm of foreign political and economic policy and in the determination of their domestic and institutional structure.

Even in this more circumscribed area, it is not

clear at what point, if any, the Soviet leaders would resort to force to keep a communist regime in line. The putative situation would involve too many unknown factors to make prediction advisable. The behavior of the United States itself, ostensibly more permissive with regard to areas near its borders, has been ambiguous. On the one hand, it was reluctant to engage in a wholesale invasion of Cuba, which resulted in the Bay of Pigs fiasco, but on the other hand it did not hesitate to commit troops for its own political objectives in the Dominican Republic. Why should the Soviet Union, which has as vital a stake in Europe as does the United States in Central America, exercise greater restraint on its power? Yet Soviet acquiescence in the trend toward the independent exercise of power by its former satellites has been remarkable, and it is fascinating to speculate on the extent to which the communist states will, in this respect, proximate that of Yugoslavia.

In reviewing the situation of the communist countries from this point of view, it must be noted that Yugoslavia and Albania *are* independent communist states, having formally freed themselves of constraints governing the relations between the other European communist states and the Soviet Union. Peculiar circumstances, most notably geographical, absent in the other states contributed to the success of their revolt. Nor were Soviet occupation troops in their midst as they are today in East Germany, Poland, and Hungary. Nevertheless, neither geography nor troop displacements appear to be crucial factors limiting the indigenous exercise of power.

One of the overriding Soviet concerns is that the

Eastern European communist states remain aligned with it in the realm of foreign policy. The key to Gomulka's rapport with Khrushchev after their unfriendly confrontation in 1956 was his obeisance to Soviet foreign policy and to Soviet policy in the international communist movement while pursuing his own domestic concerns in some practical dealings with the peasants and the church. But Poland, more than any other communist state except East Germany (whose status will remain essentially that of a satellite until some new European arrangement is worked out), must coordinate its foreign policy with that of the USSR in order to secure its frontier, which had been extended westward at the expense of defeated Germany. Polish history would suggest that in any case Poland's survival depends on alignment with Russia, or at least with either Germany or Russia. At the present time, with the refusal of West Germany to recognize the Oder-Neisse boundary, Poland has no choice except to coordinate with the USSR. It may be surmised that Gomulka's rather rapid acceptance of the Brezhnev-Kosygin regime which ousted Khrushchev may have been influenced by a reassurance that there would be no change in Soviet support for Poland's western territories.

Apart from Poland, Bulgaria (which has traditionally been closely aligned with Russia), and the exceptional case of East Germany, none of the European communist states have traditional foreign policy interests that would bind them to Soviet policy. If there are foreign policy problems, they would tend to weaken ties with the Soviet Union—for example, trade relations with the West or the development of irredentist movements such as the Transylvanian in Rumania. Yet, paradoxically, the pursuit of a greater measure of independence by the leaders of the European communist states, which would tend to bring them into closer alignment with the West, might eventually lead to their extinction at home. The cases of Albania and Yugoslavia suggest that this need not be so. Circumstances, certainly, in these countries are special: Tito is a genuinely national hero, and what occurs in the years after his death will represent a more accurate indication of the trend. Albania is run along the lines of oriental despotism. Yet the Rumanian communist leaders have shown their independence in both domestic and foreign affairs, seemingly without jeopardizing their positions. In the loosening of political controls and the amelioration of economic conditions in Eastern Europe, the tendency is to accentuate the pragmatic at the expense of the ideological. The exercise of economic autonomy vitiates Soviet plans for communist integration, a by-product of which would have been effective Soviet control, and further cripples communist ideological solidarity. A parallel exercise of autonomy in foreign affairs is limited by the relative unimportance of the part these countries could play and by the Soviet threshold of tolerance, which, precisely because it is not accurately known, is risky to test.

OTHER COMMUNIST STATES

Each of the remaining communist states represents a unique type of relationship. The closest parallel with the European relationship is the case of North Korea, which the Soviet Union would like to have serve as a buffer against non-communist influence on the mainland and also as a buffer against Communist China. The appearance of North Korea as a loyal Soviet satellite governed by hand-picked Soviet leaders has changed in the course of the Korean War and with the assertion of Chinese independence to the point where it can claim to be independent in fact. It can insure its claim by playing off Communist China against the USSR and can command the support of both in the event of conflict with South Korea and its American backers. North Korea's identification with the international communist movement would then appear to be a function of its national interest as seen at the particular moment. Its alternatives appear to be association with either the tendency led by the Soviet Union or that led by China but not the severance of relations with both. This obvious point is made to add to the argument that the independence of the communist parties cannot be equated with the abandonment of all forms of international communist ties. With North Korea, more than with the Eastern European communist states, the Sino-Soviet split has worked to its benefit, increasing its maneuverability and range of choice.

North Vietnam is outside the Soviet sphere of influence, and its gravitation away from close association with the USSR represents a breach in ideological solidarity and a lessening in the world influence of the Soviet Union but no threat to its security. For Ho Chi Minh, the astute leader of the Indo-Chinese Communists, the Sino-Soviet split has worked to his advantage (as it has for Kim Il-sung in North Korea), but he cannot, even if he so desired, break off connections with communist internationalism. His maneuverability is determined by the aim to unify Vietnam and extend communist influence in Indo-China. It is also governed by the desire to limit China's influence in his area precisely while he must rely on Chinese support to accomplish his aims. To some extent his strategy is abetted by playing off the Russians against the Chinese, but the limitation on this gambit derives from the fixed objective in South Vietnam and the unwillingness of the USSR to become too intimately involved because the area does not affect its vital interests and it wishes to maintain a *détente* atmosphere with the United States. Once again, then, independence does not connote a break with communist internationalism but rather a choice of association in an international movement determined by the national interest, at least until the United States or its powerful allies can be looked to as alternatives.

Cuba represents still another situation. This is the one communist country in which the communist revolution was not made by Communists and in which power is not held by a communist leader but by a bourgeois intellectual who became a Communist for reasons of state power. As a charismatic personality, by definition organizationally unreliable, Castro cannot inspire much confidence in the Soviet leadership. Cuba is not vital to Soviet interests, although it serves as a delicious irritant in Soviet-American relations and may be regarded as a Soviet *point d'appui* against the United States. The price the Russians pay for the maintenance of Cuba as a communist state is high in money and in aggravation. Its continuation as a communist state may not be as important to Khrushchev's successors as might be thought, partly because they inherited the results of an action they seem to have disapproved and, more to the point, because of the drain on monetary and technical resources. In return for their assistance the Russians could not even command the support of Castro on the nuclear test ban treaty or, for some time, even get him to side clearly with them against the Chinese. To Castro the problem of proletarian internationalism does not exist in traditional form. The problem of nationalism or autonomy versus internationalism does not take the form it does with the other parties. To him the existence of the Soviet Union was the guarantee of Cuba's viability as an independent state in the teeth of United States opposition. The Sino-Soviet dispute played into his hands by egging Khrushchev on to more risky policies which gave Castro missiles and by tying the Russians to him for fear the Chinese would step in *in loco parentis*. Until American diplomacy can persuade the Russians to cut their losses and leave Cuba to its own devices, Castro has a pretty good thing going.

The Cuban relationship to the international communist movement is *sui generis* and therefore from one point of view not revealing as to the fate of the movement and the idea of internationalism. Nevertheless, taking into account political and ideological developments in the underdeveloped areas, the Castro experience suggests that a new relationship within a Soviet-led movement could develop. This might take the form of an associative membership in which the individual parties and states maintain a solidarity but which is not bound by the iron rules of Stalinist inter-

nationalism or the compulsions of proletarian internationalism as it existed before the Sino-Soviet split. But
here speculation must rest.

The Chinese Communists' bid for leadership in the
international communist movement is predicated on
the revival of the idea of World Revolution in the new
revolutionary milieu of the second half of the twentieth century. By defining new revolutionary perspectives and attempting to instill a revolutionary *élan* into
the movement, the Chinese seek to assume the mantle
of authority carried by the Soviet Union since the
1920s. There is a persuasiveness in the Chinese accu-
sation that the Soviet Union and the communist movement under the latter's influence have drifted away
from a revolutionary orientation and that, contrary to
Soviet analyses, objective conditions do favor the
spread of revolutionary communism. Yet even if the
Chinese are correct in their charges that the Russians
have downgraded revolution, objective conditions have
altered so drastically that revolution in a Marxist or
quasi-Marxist sense of World Revolution seems out of
date. What the Chinese are apparently banking on is
the development of communist revolution in the underdeveloped areas which may be sufficient for the
purpose of resuscitating the revolutionary orientation
of the communist movement. They may also speculate
that successful communist action in the underdeveloped areas may in the long run revive the revolutionary potential in the West.

The historical parallel that comes readily to mind
is the split in the international socialist movement
between those who no longer seriously believed in
the Marxian revolutionary confrontation between pro-

letariat and bourgeoisie in the advanced capitalist countries and those who were willing to force the revolution, so to speak, in the name of the proletariat. This was the split—to simplify—between the Marxist tendencies represented by both the "determinists" and the evolutionary socialists of the Bernstein persuasion, on the one hand, and the Bolsheviks, who gave pride of place to the revolution itself, on the other. The idea of proletarian revolution as envisioned by Marx was transformed by his Russian disciples into revolution in a semi-industrialized country engineered in the name of the proletariat, a revolution held in trust for the proletariat by the communist party. The Chinese Communists' revolution went one step further: it took place in a backward, agrarian country, yet its leaders still maintained the myth of proletarian revolution. It could nevertheless be argued that the Chinese revolution was thoroughly Leninist, if the essence of Leninism lies in the concept of a communist party staffed by professional revolutionaries dedicated to the proposition of effecting a revolution from above. Under this line of reasoning, the class composition of the masses engaged in revolution is immaterial. Whether proletarians or peasants, they are led by intellectuals or intelligentsia drawn from strata of the bourgeoisie who seek power to build a "socialist" society in the name of the workers.

If there is then an organic ideological and institutional connection between the Bolshevik and Chinese revolutions, there is nevertheless a disjunction caused by the vastly different socioeconomic conditions out of which new societies were to be created. What the Bolsheviks could accomplish in a relatively brief span is denied to the Chinese Communists, for whom problems of industrialization and agricultural production are infinitely more complex. The time span will be longer and the measure of accomplishment less. This has already led the Chinese to experiment with new institutions, such as the ill-starred communes, as a means of accelerating production and, at the same time, of communizing society. The less favorable economic situation has also led the Chinese to expect more of their communist brethren in the way of mutual aid and mutual sacrifice. Communist solidarity implies that the better-endowed communist states should be willing to sacrifice a portion of their largesse to aid the less-developed communist countries. However adequate the communist states might have thought their aid to China—and communist aid, though considerable, was not of the order to help China with any sort of breakthrough—the Chinese did not find it sufficient.

In their conflict with the Soviet Union, the Chinese Communists faced two orders of problems: how to relate as Communists and how to develop their resources. In the search for communist and non-communist allies, the Chinese found a greater identification of interest with the underdeveloped areas than with the communist movement *per se,* and this for good reason. The parties in the advanced capitalist countries, without revolutionary prospects, find the USSR's perspectives of peaceful coexistence with the West and avoidance of force and violence closer to their interests. What the Chinese Communist orientation offers them is the consolation that if they jeopardize their positions in militant and uncompromising behavior, they will at least suffer their losses as good revolution-

ary Communists. Since with few exceptions these parties are reluctant to martyr themselves and see, moreover, no compelling reason for doing so, the prospects
of the Chinese for reconstituting communist internationalism are limited from the start. Whatever prospects the Chinese do have along these lines seem to
emerge from their self-identification with the underdeveloped areas, but once again the limitations on the
development of communist allies are apparent.

UNDERDEVELOPED COUNTRIES:
CHINESE AND SOVIET POLICY

If conditions in the underdeveloped areas are more
propitious for the Chinese, they nevertheless suggest
that communism will no longer develop in the old
way. The Comintern had been made up of communist
parties, often powerless sects, none of which held state
power except in the Soviet Union. Moreover, in the
underdeveloped areas controlled by the metropolitan
powers, the communist movements were often the only
radical alternative to the existing power structure. In
many cases the parties and their trade unions were
extensions of the communist movement in the mother
country, as, for example, the *Rassemblement démo-
cratique africain* (R. D. A.) in French West Africa
and the communist movement in the British West
Indies. With the coming of independence, the non-
communist nationalist movements, by and large, have
become the dominant revolutionizing force, and, moreover, the one-party state has emerged as a distinguish-
ing feature of these new countries. Not only have the
communist movements failed to achieve a greater

measure of power in this new environment—again with certain exceptions, as in Cuba—but they have in a number of cases been weakened and suppressed, as they were in Egypt. Failure and suppression do not necessarily mean that the adhesion and loyalty to a communist international have been weakened; quite the contrary, the parties may feel all the stronger need for association in an international. What is at issue, however, is whether the communist parties of the underdeveloped areas will, merely being so located, align themselves with the Chinese. What is even more crucial is the alignment of the nationalist regimes themselves and particularly of the radical nationalist one-party states.

Soviet policy since the Second Comintern Congress in 1920 has fluctuated between the poles of support for communist revolutionary movements in the underdeveloped areas and support for the native revolutionary movements against the foreign occupier conceived as a "stage," a steppingstone on the way to the achievement of proletarian revolution. The decision as to choice of strategy for the indigenous communist movement was more often than not a function of Soviet policy toward the area concerned. Local communist interests were often sacrificed to reasons of state and rationalized as a contribution to the common good— that is, to the interests of the Soviet Union as the standard-bearer of World Revolution. Communist strategy toward the colonial (underdeveloped) areas remained remarkably fixed both in its alternatives and its generalized application until relatively recently— that is, until Khrushchev's rise to power and the growth of the independence movement in Africa, to whose social structure traditional communist class analysis hardly applied. Soviet theorists have accordingly developed a more flexible concept to accommodate the new situation, positing the idea of "national democratic state" as one of the more important avenues to the goal of socialist revolution. The concept concedes the leadership of the national revolutionary movements to the native non-communist leadership which carries the states through two stages of development: first political independence from the metropolitan power, and then economic independence from the capitalist powers, which hopefully will lead the new states onto the road of "socialism." The role of the Communists is to assist these national democratic tendencies, not to displace them, at least not prematurely.

This strategy is in line with the possibilities in many areas where the communist movements are too weak in any case to lead a revolutionary struggle on their own or to attempt to seize power in "national democratic" states—such as Ghana, Guinea, and Mali. The strategy also accords with the evolutionary and peaceful-coexistence prospectus of the Twentieth CPSU Congress. By playing down the revolutionary role of the communist movements in these areas, the Soviet Union is able to maneuver its policy toward these states without embarrassment. If, moreover, these states take the non-capitalist road to development and proclaim a socialist system of sorts, their ideological orientation will point toward the communist, not the capitalist, states. The dilemma, or perhaps the hopeful prospect, is that a new form of revolutionary internationalism will develop, not with communist parties

themselves bound by ties of proletarian internationalism but with ideologically compatible state entities
bound by ties of economic and foreign-policy interests.
For the Soviet Union, for example, this would represent an accretion of world influence that could not be
attained if it chose exclusively to support the indigenous communist movements. The local Communists'
reward would come in assisting the new states as technical and organizational experts (so often in short
supply in the underdeveloped areas), and in carrying
the World Revolution, re-evaluated, forward.

Soviet strategy in the underdeveloped areas places
the Chinese Communists in a dilemma in regard to
their attempts to counter the Soviet Union in the
communist movement and in the underdeveloped
areas. With little prospect of winning over the communist parties in the advanced countries to their side,
the Chinese have converted the reality into a principle
by proclaiming revolution in the underdeveloped areas
as the main consideration of the communist movement.
This position is taken directly in opposition to the Soviet Union, which has proclaimed peaceful coexistence
between capitalist and communist states as the main
strategic concern of the present historical period and
formulated its strategy in the underdeveloped areas on
this basis. But if the Chinese Communists focus on
the underdeveloped areas, to what precisely do they
turn? To the communist movements or to the native
revolutionary forces and the nationalist states? As a
non-ruling communist party, the Chinese could perhaps have given their uninhibited support to the communist movements without sacrificing much of consequence. But precisely because they are a state, they

are influenced by some of the basic considerations that guide the Soviet Union and, for that matter, any state, no matter what its ideological persuasion. Like the Soviet Union, the Chinese must choose to support either the indigenous communist party or the national revolutionary movement. Only rarely, as in Indonesia, did the interests of the two coincide so closely as to obviate the necessity of choice. Chinese association with non-communist revolutionary groups or states *a priori* limits their activity in directly promoting communist revolution. In principle, then—and the Soviet rift cannot sidestep quarrel over principle—there would be no difference between the Soviet and Chinese positions.

The Chinese have moved into the underdeveloped areas proclaiming their identity of interests as an underdeveloped state—but one that knows how to industrialize—and as a non-white one. But the pay-off is not in the self-proclaimed image but in the nature of the product for sale. China has an ideology, technicians, technical assistance, and goods. The USSR has more. For the new states, the competition between the Soviet and Chinese Communists provides a new bargaining position, heretofore confined to a choice between assistance from capitalists and the communist "bloc." The situation then provides the Chinese with some footholds that develop as a result of bargaining between the underdeveloped country and the Soviet Union. The Chinese can move in where the Russians refuse to go or are unwilling to commit themselves. It is also conceivable that the Chinese will be closer to certain foreign-policy interests of the new states than the Russians might be. But essentially the

Chinese, no less than the Russians, would be guided by state interests in dealing with these new countries, and it is difficult to see how the Chinese have more leverage than the Russians. To push speculation, the formation of an international based on the principle of underdeveloped versus developed states, including the communist states of Europe, would appear to be a suicidal move for most of the underdeveloped countries. If the exercise of power in these states depends on the satisfaction of aspirations, as we are so often told, assistance from the advanced countries is indispensable. The Chinese could implement their revolutionary line in these underdeveloped states only at the expense of jeopardizing their relations with the ruling groups. This is precisely the situation of the Soviet Union.

To revert by way of summary to the propositions advanced at the beginning of this book, authority in the international communist movement, embodied in the idea of World Revolution, was vested in the Soviet Union by a process of sublimation. In the 1920s, with the fading prospects of revolutions other than the Soviet, the revolutionary Soviet state remained the one hope for the furthering of the revolutionary movement. Manipulated for the national interests of the Soviet state by Stalin, and later by Khrushchev, who made peaceful coexistence of competing social systems the major tenet of his international strategy, the movement was transformed by and large into a mere political instrument of Soviet policy. This was the situation of the movement, apparent to all, but not until the 1960s was it openly criticized from within the movement by those who were prepared to challenge Moscow's authority and were backed by the paraphernalia of state power. The Chinese Communists' challenge to the Soviet leaders is in essence a bid for authority in the international movement on the basis of their policy which they identify with World Revolution—that is, with the revolutionary interests of the communist parties as a whole.

The effect of the Sino-Soviet quarrel is clear and devastating; communism as an organized unitary movement has ceased to exist. National communist parties remain and international communist action and even organization continue to exist, but the distinctive feature of the old institution has disappeared; that is, there is no longer an association of national communist parties, linked to one another and to a center to which is entrusted the interpretation of doctrine and the strategic policies derived from—or rationalized through —the doctrine as interpreted by one party. The extent to which international institutional arrangements have degenerated may be appreciated by noting that no formal mechanism now exists for recognizing (legitimatizing) the establishment of a communist party. Who decides? Instead, two centers, two state powers, are competing for authority over the international movement, one on the basis of a fundamentalist revolutionary doctrine and the other on the basis of a reformist or class-conciliationist doctrine. Neither the Soviet nor the Chinese Communists have been able to advance an acceptable principle on the basis of which the international movement can be organized. Both parties disclaim the intention of assuming the role of a command party. Both proclaim that all parties are equal.

The Soviet Communists advance the organizing principle of majority rule, which is unacceptable to the Chinese because they are so far from agreement with the Soviet leaders on major aspects of policy. Majority rule is also held suspect by those parties which, though sympathetic to Soviet policy, fear the possibility of resubordination as a consequence of binding decisions acceptable to a majority which Moscow can still command. The Chinese, by contrast, suggest as the organizing principle unanimity, which is unobtainable precisely because the interests of the various parties—not only the Chinese—are diverse and because certain of the parties are willing to fight openly for their preferences. It may be surmised that the Soviet and Chinese Communists would settle for recognition of their authority in a looser and more flexible organization than has heretofore existed, but even if this could be attained—which seems unlikely—an international so constituted might very well resemble the ineffectual organization of the socialist international, a sort of platonic international.

The prospect of a revived international embracing all units of the communist movement is, then, remote; the prospect of two competing communist orbits, each with a less formalized relationship than had existed in the past seems more likely (with, possibly, loosely structured regional groupings in each). But this will not be the internationalism of Marx, of an international association bound by class interests and proletarian solidarity. The pattern appears to be more nearly one of competing alliance systems based on national or particularist interests. What the future development will be, however, is not merely a function of communist interests and ideas alone. Just as the movement in the past has been shaped by the interaction of communist and non-communist policies, so the future in some degree will be shaped by the policies of the West, most notably of the United States. Just as, for example, Soviet-Chinese relations were influenced by Soviet-American policies during World War Two and later by the decision of the United States not to recognize Communist China, so American policy will bear on the possibilities of dissolution or reformation of the communist world. Part II of the book is therefore devoted to a consideration of American policy toward the international communist movement.

PART II

United States Policy and World Communism

6. THE IDEOLOGICAL ISSUE

American scholarly and journalistic writing on the Soviet Union and international communism has been preoccupied with communist ideology and its relation to policy. Probably the single most influential such exercise was George F. Kennan's "X" article, "The Sources of Soviet Conduct," published in *Foreign Affairs*, July 1947, which derived a policy of "containment" of the USSR from the author's reading of communist ideology.[1] Kennan himself was shortly to criticize the Truman Doctrine as an operational implementation of his views,[2] though it appeared that this military facet of American policy nicely complemented the politicoeconomic Marshall Plan designed to contain Soviet policy in Western Europe. Moreover, Kennan's concern with the ideological basis of policy seemed to have receded by the time he made his talks on "disengagement," delivered as the BBC Reith lectures in 1957.[3]

If Kennan's views on the relation between communist ideology and policy appear ambiguous or have simply changed over time, other commentators have presented consistent positions which have sharply conflicted one with another: that ideology is the key to both Soviet domestic and foreign policy; that ideology is operative in domestic but not in foreign policy; that ideology no longer has any bearing on domestic affairs but is the key to foreign policy; and, less frequently, that the conduct of Soviet foreign policy is traditional.[4] Perhaps the most exasperating position is that which maintains that ideology cannot be separated from Soviet policy—exasperating because it is a true and at the same time meaningless statement. Ideology is always a component of policy in any state, just as values permeate the actions of individuals and groups at a lower level in society. What is crucial—and has most often been dealt with most inadequately—is precisely which ideological components influence, shape, or determine foreign policy. What, to take the most hoary example, does the idea of the inevitable victory of communism over capitalism have to do with Khrushchev's attempt to reach an accommodation with the United States or with the signing of the test ban treaty? What, on the other side, did American "free world" ideology have to do with its response to the Hungarian revolt and its suppression by the Russians?

The relationship between ideology and foreign policy is complex and often unknowable. Since it is the feelings and motives of the principal actors which are often crucial, without the aid of the psychoanalytic couch the determining factors in policy-making may elude analysis. Yet it can be argued that the Communists have invited the preoccupation of their antagonists with communist ideology. Flaunting a theory of world revolution and an ideology codified during the

Stalinist era, the Communists have asked to be taken at their word, as it were. Beyond this, and more important, preoccupation in the United States with communist ideology has served to minimize attention to Soviet *behavior*. Soviet action that appeared to be reasonable was placed in the context of world revolutionary and expansionist aims, thus reducing what the Communists did to the status of a strategem unworthy of serious response. Thus, preoccupation with communist ideology has served not so much as a means of comprehending Soviet foreign policy as a cover, conscious or unconscious, for American policy. Viewed in the perspective of fifty years, American policy has wavered between the alternatives, starkly put, of facing the Soviet Union simply as a national power or facing it as a mere component of international communism. More often than not, American policy and attitudes have been molded by ideological anti-communism rather than by the pragmatism on which Americans pride themselves.

In contrast to the attention paid to communist ideology, analysis of the influence of American ideology on United States foreign policy has been neglected. While, it has been said, "our foreign relations grow out of, and are expressive of, our entire national life," democracy has no dogma, no orthodoxy.[5] Indeed, a codified American ideology does not exist, its absence giving rise to some concern that democracy is at a disadvantage relative to communism, which has been able to set forth a neat package of its beliefs. Yet the absence of a codified ideology does not mean that ideology does not exist; it means rather that it is more difficult to agree on the content of the belief system and, particularly, to isolate and to analyze the operative elements of the ideology.[6] Failure to do so has led to a distorted picture of Soviet-American relations and has colored the entire history of American policy toward the Soviet Union and world communism. To Americans, the Soviet Union is the enemy—aggressive, expansionist, and committed to the destruction of American and all other free society. In self-defense, Americans, who would prefer to tend their own gardens, are compelled to resist this proclaimed menace with all the resources at their command, shielding whatever country from communist subversion and opposing the Communists at every turn. This is the myth. What is not acknowledged is the dynamic nature of American policy, the pursuit of its own imperial ambitions, and its attempt to structure the world to its own liking, with the communist issue serving more often than not merely as an excuse for policy. In the measured language of the diplomatic historian:

The confrontation of America and Russia in 1917-19 was not merely abrupt, it was accompanied by two contending programs for a new world order, programs derived not from the international arena alone but also from the preoccupations and perspectives of two continental societies *situated on the margins of Europe*[7] [*emphasis added*].

This is not to argue that the United States should not attempt to fashion a world compatible with its interests; the point is rather that the policies pursued over the past fifteen years have flown in the face of historical trends and political realities. Events in Latin America and Asia in the 1960s are clear testimony to the failure of American policy both in conception and execution. Preference for the myth rather than actual Soviet policy and actual communist capability has inhibited the development of a foreign policy harmonious with the times, when it has not led into blind alleys.

ACCEPTANCE OF THE COMMUNIST MYTH

Viewed in the perspective of fifty years, the American attitude toward world communism has been a mirror image of the Soviet attitude toward world capitalism. Whereas it has totally rejected the Marxian analysis of capitalism, class conflict, and proletarian revolution, United States policy has proceeded as if the Marxian *Weltanschauung* were true and, moreover, the proper object of foreign policy. When the Bolshevik revolution hailed the split of world capitalism into two competing social systems, with the capitalists doomed to destruction, the United States accepted the challenge. Its policy from the first—whatever the waverings of Woodrow Wilson—was based on ideological grounds, and its aim was to destroy the Bolshevik regime. The flavor of the American attitude was conveyed in the remarks of the American ambassador to Russia, who wrote on November 8, 1917: "It is reported that the Petrograd Council of Workmen and Soldiers has named a Cabinet with Lenin as Premier, Trotsky as Minister of Foreign Affairs and Madame or Mlle. Kollontai as Minister of Education. Disgusting. . . . Of course, we would not, or I would not, recognize any Ministry of which Lenin is Premier or

Trotsky Minister of Foreign Affairs."[8] Although there were substantial arguments for American participation in the Allied intervention in Russia on non-ideological grounds—to limit Japanese expansion, to safeguard military stores at Murmansk and Archangel, and to assist the Czech Legion to cross Siberia to join the Entente on the Western front—the underlying hope, as was pointed out in Part I, was that the presence of American troops would encourage the Russian people to establish a democratic form of government—that is, to overthrow the Bolsheviks. Revolution in Russia or in East-Central Europe was simply not on the dockets of the victorious powers.

The ideological basis of American policy toward the Soviet Union has been its constant factor, despite recognition and the World War Two association. From the outset, the American government established to its satisfaction the identity of interests between the Comintern—the international revolutionary movement —and the Soviet state and because of the revolutionary nature of the new state refused to establish normal intercourse with it until 1933. The analysis was of course correct. No special powers of divination were required to establish the connection between the Comintern and the Bolshevik government. The appeal for the convocation of the first Comintern Congress was issued through the Soviet foreign office. The Soviet state openly appropriated money for world-wide revolutionary activities. This was the period when the Bolsheviks conceived of the foreign office as subordinate to the Comintern—that is, to world, or at least European, revolutionary strategy. The situation was soon reversed, with the Comintern becoming an ad-

junct of the state. The formal separation of the activities of the two was the signal that the Bolshevik leaders
realized that they too had to play the game according
to traditional rules. If they could also manage to get
the support of communist parties of other countries
by direction or indirection, so much the better. In
short, Bolshevik policy adjusted more or less quickly
to the requirement that it exist in a hostile capitalist
environment. In contrast, American policy did not
acknowledge the legal existence of the Soviet state. As
the stronger power, the United States could afford to
feed its ideological conceptions. The poor, the ex-
ploited, and the weak cannot indulge their prejudices
as freely as the strong. The Bolsheviks, for whom the
acquisition of full sovereignty, national security, and
a going economy was a paramount consideration, came
to employ their world revolutionary ideas largely as
back-up or cover for the construction of a Soviet Socialist Republic. The United States chose to ignore
the actuality for the myth, regarding revolution in
general and the Bolshevik revolution in particular as
disruptive of a policy of shaping the world according
to its own ideological preferences.

The underlying consistency of the American attitude
is reflected in the refusal to recognize the Soviet government for sixteen years and the failure to accord
recognition to the Chinese Communist government
established in 1949. (The United States recognized
the Franco government within days after the capture
of Madrid in 1939.) The ideological bias of American
policy toward communism comes through in even
sharper focus when compared to policy toward the
fascist and Nazi powers. While there was a marked

distaste for fascism in the United States, the government nevertheless did not sever relations with the fascist powers nor did it effectively oppose them until they declared war on the United States. American attitudes up to (say) 1939 were shaped less by power considerations than by ideological conceptions. Soviet policy in the interwar period was essentially defensive; Nazi policy, by contrast, was outspokenly revisionist and expansionist. The stated objective of world domination was as clear in *Mein Kampf* as in any programmatic statement of the Bolsheviks. The crucial difference was that, as ideologically revisionist and aggressive as the Nazis were, they did not—in contrast to the Communists—threaten the existing capitalist order. A Nazi policy of limited ambitions would not have been incompatible with American interests; Soviet policy, which hardly conflicted with American policy interests in the interwar period, was anathema because of anticapitalist communist doctrine. The United States may have been entitled to its anti-Bolshevik bias; that is not the crux of the matter. The point is that its policy toward world communism and Soviet Russia was thus ideologically determined, thereby accepting the communist analysis of the world situation. This contributed to the hardening of Bolshevik patterns and to the rigidification of intercommunist relations during the interwar period. How cause was related to effect cannot be determined with any precision. Yet the American obsession with the ideological precepts of communism takes on all the earmarks of tragedy when it is recognized that the stability of Europe and any effective opposition to Nazi power lay in coming to terms with the Soviet Union and acknowledging its security interests in Eurasia, which coincided with rather than ran counter to American interests.

THE PRICE OF ANTICOMMUNISM

Ideological anticommunism has also taken its toll in American society, contributing to the stifling of independent thought and critical discussion on both foreign and domestic policy. The obsession with communism—or better, with the dangers of communism—in this the most advanced industrial and most powerful military power in the world is outside the realm of reasonable behavior. The hysteria that developed over the activities of a motley group of Bolsheviks after World War One and over the alleged influence of American Communists after World War Two was in inverse ratio to the threat posed to American security. Communist power represented by the Soviet Union and the Comintern in the interwar period did not threaten the United States in any vital way. It was only after World War Two, when the Soviet Union emerged as the major power on the European continent, that the United States and the USSR came into serious political conflict. Underlying the clash of interests was the ideological animus against communism which was transformed into an operational principle. If Russia in 1945 had been Czarist instead of communist, there still would inevitably have been attempts to contain its power. The new ingredient which made a qualitative difference was the investment of the clash of interests with ideological fervor, giving it the character of a holy war—on both sides. The United

States was permeated by an unthinking anticommunism that penetrated all aspects of American society. The portrait of the Soviet Union presented by government, private groups, and academe alike was that of a monolithic, totalitarian society, incapable of change, outwardly aggressive, and supported by tightly controlled communist parties bent on subversion of the established order. In short, appearance was separated from reality, word from deed. The word for purposes of action became the deed. The effect in the United States was not merely hostility to a foreign power that presumably threatened American vital interests, but a *Gleichschaltung* of opinion. Dissent was stifled. Criticism became suspect. Government functionaries were routinized. Students—and professors—became silent. Bipartisanism in foreign policy—that is, the agreement not to disagree—was raised to the level of a principle. (That such domestic policies as medical care for the aged or equality before the law for all American citizens may legitimately be regarded as the subject of bitter partisan activity while dissent on foreign policy that may lead to waste, destruction, and war is regarded as unpatriotic, if not virtually treasonous partisanship, can be understood only in the context of the pervading irrationality of American society.) Consensus became the ruling principle of American society—that is, agreement with the ideas of the established order.

No doubt there are many explanations for the development of this conformistic, intolerant society. There is unquestionably a great hostility to all that communism represents, just as there was to Nazism. But anti-Nazism never approached the level of intensity of anticommunism in this country, and the Germany that precipitated the war quickly became our best friend and ally with little opposition. The grooming of the former enemy as the pivot of our Atlantic policy might be justified on the basis of *Machtpolitik,* though there were other alternatives. But the smoothness of the relationship betokens something else, an ideological affinity stemming from comparable economic and social orders. Similarly, the quasi-paranoid hostility to communism reflects a deep-set anxiety in American society, first implicitly challenged by the Bolshevik revolution and subsequently by the outbreak of communist and other revolutions throughout the world. For American society, ideological pretentions aside, is deeply resistant to radical change. The only revolution it believes in is the Revolution of 1776, and that only because it is in the past.

The United States of America has achieved a more perfect union—its contours apparently have only to be rounded out somewhat by the Great Society—and it intends to conserve it. Industrial capitalism of the nineteenth century has reached a peak in monopolistic, corporate American capitalism, which has produced the strongest economic and military power in the world. The material welfare of the country—despite "pockets of poverty"—needs no elaboration. Progress in this respect has been an ever-rising curve, achieved, moreover, relatively peacefully within the constitutional framework. This is no mean social achievement. The productive capacity of the United States, understandably a source of pride to Americans, is at the same time a source of envy and emulation for the Soviet Communists. Communists recognize that the American productive potential is the indispensable basis which Marx envisioned as the precondition for the establishment of the good society. What is less appreciated is that this advanced industrial society is subversive of the moral and political principles associated with constitutional democracy: a genuine tolerance for differing views and values, or the idea that the human being is an end in himself and not an instrument to be manipulated by state or society. That is to say, a tremendous gap has developed between the principles on which the American society was founded and the existing reality. The gap between myth and reality is, in turn, one of the significant factors affecting the conduct of foreign policy. American society has become permeated by a "false consciousness," to borrow from Marx's conception of ideology, which it employs to justify its role in the world. The deceit and manipulation which have come to permeate domestic society are at the same time externalized in attitudes toward foreign affairs, and the resulting "requirements" of foreign policy are used to reinforce the domestic ideological straitjacket. The contradiction between professed principles and public attitudes and official actions creates a double standard which feeds foreign suspicion and encourages cynical appraisal of American foreign policy.

THE AMERICAN ATTITUDE TOWARD REVOLUTION

The attitude of the United States toward revolution provides a leading example of the discrepancy between its professions and its behavior. The year 1776 celebrates the right of a people to revolt and to order its society as it sees fit. The principle of self-determination, associated with Woodrow Wilson (and, properly speaking, with the Bolsheviks too), broadly conceived implied the right of a people to make its own choices even to the point of social revolution. Perhaps there is no finer expression of the democratic ethos than these rights to revolution and self-determination, implying a tolerance, patience, and humor in observing other peoples express their political and socioeconomic preferences. Political principles are not eternal, but the rights of revolution and of self-determination seem more relevant now, after the break-up of the colonial system affecting the larger portion of humanity, than they were after World War One, when self-determination applied largely to the multi-states of Europe. There certainly appears to be appreciation in the United States of the contemporary relevance of revolution. It is expressed in the American vocabulary— as, for instance, the "revolution of rising expectations," —but, as might be expected, with a connotation of consumer goods rather than political action. (Not that there is anything to despise in people's wanting goods, but Americans have a tendency to project their own values onto others to whom the "revolution of rising expectations" may signify merely the acquisition of the means to keep people from starving over a foreseeable future.) In short, those principles which have become part of the American myth are precisely the ones which are rejected in practice. It is not only communist revolution which Americans deplore and actively oppose but revolutions in general.

There is no mystery surrounding the American distaste for revolution. As a rich, powerful, and sated power, the United States does not care to see the international order disrupted by upheavals which bring to power groups antagonistic to United States interests. Revolution, as many American policy-makers, if not the American public at large, understand, is almost by definition hostile to the United States, because of its socioeconomic implications, or its "anti-colonial" character, which includes the United States whether or not it cares to be associated with the imperialist powers, or simply because the United States has established a reputation as a reactionary force. But there is a particular connection between communist revolution and revolution in general, which is pertinent but which has not received much explicit elaboration by students of American foreign policy. Stated simply, this is the tendency to identify all revolutions with communism and moreover to regard revolutions as bad or hostile to our interests.

The Bolshevik revolution was so disturbing to American leaders not merely because it took Russia out of the war or because it was a revolution in Russia but more significantly because it symbolized the general feeling of revolt against the existing order.[9] The new international order which was supposed to follow the establishment of the peace did not contemplate the radicalization of the European social structure. The tendency grew, therefore, to identify all revolutionary agitation with Bolshevism. Moreover, communist revolution came to have a rather special character in comparison to revolutions of the past. Revolution was no longer considered an indigenous phenomenon but was regarded rather as an extension of Soviet policy. This conception was fed by the bolshevization of the Comintern and its structuring as an association of national units under the direct control of Moscow. Leninist-Stalinist doctrine on the élitist character of the communist parties and the centralization of the movement contributed further to this conception. The fact that there was an inverse relationship between communist propaganda on revolution and the ability of the Communists to mount a successful revolution at any time during the interwar period had no effect on the myth-making. With the establishment of communist regimes in East-Central Europe after World War Two, communist revolution lost any legitimacy it might have had and came to be regarded strictly as a conspiratorial-manipulative action imposing the will of a small group of men on an unwilling people either through internal subversion or external *force de main*. If, as in the Vietminh revolution against the French, the Titoist struggle against the Nazis, or the Chinese Communist civil war against the Nationalists, the Communists are conceded to have come to power independently of Moscow, the legitimacy of the revolution is still denied on the grounds of organizational connection and self-determination, new style. That is, the three revolutions just mentioned aligned themselves with "international communism," at least for a time, and the victorious Communists imposed oppressive regimes on the people who had collaborated with them in the revolutionary struggle. Even when it became clear that these states were not under the control of Moscow or "international communism," they were still, in different measure, regarded as pariahs.

If the issue of revolution was important to American policy-makers during the interwar period, it is doubly of concern today when all the world outside the ad-

vanced countries is caught up in discontent with the
prevailing order, and the new states in particular are
searching for appropriate ways of developing their societies—and when the United States has taken upon
itself responsibility for world order. It is unfortunate
for peoples attempting to break out of old patterns
that the Communists have tarnished the idea of revolution so that all revolutions are suspect in Washington by definition. Even more troublesome is the fact
that although it is possible, for the most part, to distinguish *organizationally* between communist and non-
communist nationalists, in terms of *policies* the distin-
guishing marks are fading.[10] No better example of the
ideological straitjacket in which American policy functions is afforded than the spectacle of President Johnson's dispatch of Marines to the Dominican Republic
in 1965, bolstered by the CIA's certification that there
were fifty-odd Communists among the rebel forces.
The subsequent assignment of the FBI to verify the
CIA's list, presumably to give authority to the President's action, would appear ludicrous if it were not
symptomatic of the arrogant and essentially manipulative character of American policy. To become realistic,
American policy, frozen in its ideological mold, must
recognize the right of peoples to their revolutions,
communist or otherwise. In the light of history, communism has become the agency not of the creation
of a more perfect post-capitalist society but rather
of the means of breaking out of backwardness, first
in the peculiar circumstances of the Russian experience, but more generally in the semi-agrarian countries
of the world, most notably in China. Not all such
communist or quasi-communist upheavals threaten
American security.

7. UNITED STATES REACTION TO THE COMMUNIST SCHISM

The split in the international communist movement was hailed by the experts as an event of world historic importance. If so, official Washington was unprepared for it. For that matter, so were most specialists on communism in Washington, the universities, and the press. Since prediction is not one of the strong points of the social sciences, no value judgment is intended. Yet this was not merely a matter of the inadequacy of analytical tools. Prevailing ideology enforced a disbelief that quarrel was genuine, that it was lasting and not merely a temporary aberration, and that it might have some implications for American policy. This attitude, not to be confused with the understandable exercise of elementary caution and tentative analysis, was not confined to policy-makers but extended to the experts themselves. It was rooted primarily in the prevailing view of the nature of Soviet totalitarianism and the monolithism of international communism which had previously met dissent by coercion, force, manipulation, persuasion, and other sanctions, as the situation warranted. Prevailing opinion held that the Kremlin had always succeeded in restoring the situation *ante* (the implications of the Stalin-Tito affair were curiously neglected) and that therefore a new unity would be imposed on the communist movement. This attitude, serviceable for a long period, nevertheless neglected history and the dynamic nature of politics for ideological construct. It was also weighted with the legacy of McCarthyism which discouraged the espousal of any ideas on communism that might run against the prevailing ideology. Analysis was, moreover, inhibited by the nature of bureaucracy, which places the lowest premium on the individual's ideas, subjecting them instead and deliberately to the "refinement" of clearance by section chiefs, editors, coordinators, and, not least, to the preconceptions of the officers for whom the analysis is being prepared. Responsibility is thus diffused and, in regard to communism, McCarthyism is internalized into the bureaucratic mode of operation. Nevertheless, the emergence of Sino-Soviet differences was cautiously noted, beginning in 1956, and the developing quarrel was recorded in detail by Washington analysts. Fragmentation of the communist movement at large was so amply documented that it became necessary to come to some conclusions about the meaning of the rift. Such discussion centered in the lower ranges of the bureaucracy until well after 1960 when the top echelons of the State Department seemed to become more than casually interested in the problem. Interpretations of the rift, of which some samples follow, once again reflected ideological preferences.

A major concern of the analysts was whether the Sino-Soviet rift was caused by ideological or political (national interest) factors. The very posing of the problem in this fashion reflected the stereotyped thinking about communist politics and the unreality of trying to separate ideological from political motives. Yet there was clearly a logic underlying this approach, for if the rift could be demonstrated to be essentially ideological rather than rooted in the hard facts of clashing national policies, then it could be argued— as it was in Washington—that nothing of substance had changed. The Communists were quarreling over esoteric doctrine; it was nothing to us.

Another common view was that the Sino-Soviet rift could be of no profit to the United States. Both the Russians and the Chinese, it was argued, were Communists, and any dispute they might be seized of on matters of ideology or internal or external policy was taking place within the communist framework. Since communism was by definition the enemy, it did not matter what the issues were or how they were resolved. By definition, nothing good could come of the quarrel. This was a view somewhat less rigid than the one held by a tiny minority that the Sino-Soviet rift was a put-up job, a conspiracy on the order of the Soviet-Yugoslav rift, to deceive the West which, after all had been said and done, saw a close identity of views between Yugoslav and Soviet Communists. In this vein, the Soviet-Yugoslav rapprochement under Khrushchev's dispensation was regarded less as a patching up of differences than as a stage play, bringing into public view the close relationship that had always existed under the surface.

A closely related view, and one which reflected the

"transference" of communist thinking, conceded the existence of Sino-Soviet differences but argued that there was insufficient appreciation of the role of the "dialectic" in communist affairs. That is to say, in conformity with the operations of the dialectic, Sino-Soviet differences would be synthesized and a new unity would emerge. This would occur apparently because it was so stated in textbooks and because previous differences in the communist movement had always somehow been "reconciled."

What might be called the rational view conceded and documented the rift but argued that in the end unity would prevail because the Soviet and Chinese Communists had more to lose than to gain by prolonging their quarrel. The fallacy here was in imputing a rationality to the Communists on the basis of American ideological conceptions of how the communist movement should behave.

Nevertheless, the prevailing view adopted by the Washington experts on communism was that Sino-Soviet differences were genuine and would deepen, and that the international communist movement was being fractionalized, although there remained differences of opinion over the operative causes of the dispute—for example, a lower level of Soviet aid than the Chinese had anticipated; the unwillingness of the Russians to develop a nuclear capacity for the Chinese; dissatisfaction with Soviet support for Chinese foreign policy, and conversely Chinese disinclination to follow through on the implications of Khrushchev's co-existence policy—which comes to the same thing. In any case, the implications of the development for American foreign policy could no longer be ignored. What came into question was, moreover, not merely internecine communist quarrels but the entire range of Khrushchev's policy, of which the Sino-Soviet rift was an integral part.

FOREIGN POLICY RESPONSE

Analysis and policy do not necessarily go hand in hand. Although it takes some courage to offer an analysis that runs counter to prevailing estimates, the responsibility entailed in committing the nation to a policy is of a higher order, risking, as it may, prestige, money, and lives. The personal preference of the policy-maker and the importance ascribed to domestic repercussions, moreover, may cancel out the analysis regardless whether the nation is committed to greater or lesser risk. The gap between policy and analysis is strikingly illustrated, for example, in the Bay of Pigs operation, which presumably counted on the spontaneous identification and support of the Cuban people with the invading forces precisely at the time when the prevailing and bureaucratically responsible view in Washington was that Castro commanded the support of a majority of his people. In the case of the upheaval in the communist world, it is understandable that there was a somewhat less than bullish attitude toward a revision of policy. A secular division in the communist orbit implied a refinement of American policy, the delineation of choices, and the willingness to shoulder risks of unpopularity at home while enlarging the sphere of action abroad. With mock humor the days of Stalin were nostalgically recalled, when there was—or appeared to be—certainty, the stability of a clearly defined hostility on both sides. No wonder there were statements declaring that the communist rift was an internal affair outside the influence of United States policy. These reflected a certain asperity and an inability to come to any clear-cut decisions on the matter.

One of the inferences that might have been drawn was that of the unimportance of having a policy against international communism. If, for example, the Communist Party of New Zealand, one of the components of international communism, was upset by Soviet policy and opted to throw its weight on the side of the Chinese Communists, what effect did this have on United States policy and what could it do about it anyway? The New Zealand Communist Party was properly the concern of the New Zealand government and whether the party was pro-Moscow, pro-Peking, or simply hung up was not of much political moment. The case of the New Zealand Communists can be multiplied many times over since most of the non-ruling communist parties are weak and ineffectual.[1] One could, of course, sit back and enjoy the confusion in the communist movement and the disruption of its vaunted unity, but American policy refuses to be so relaxed.

But, of more consequence to this argument, there was no longer an international communist movement against which one could have a policy even if one wanted to. The Sino-Soviet conflict signified the end of the international movement as it had hitherto existed. Fashioning a policy appropriate to the new situation required a keen analysis of the split's import and its meaning for policy. If, for example, the split was found to be caused by forces internal to the communist movement, affecting, say, domestic institutional innovations, then the conclusion might be reached that the split was immaterial to American policy, and consequently both strands of international communism, Soviet and Chinese, should receive equal treatment. If, on the other hand, the split appeared to have been caused by Soviet policy in its attempt to reach an accommodation with the United States, then obviously differentiated treatment was required. As a minimum, American policy should then avoid action that would drive the former partners together again. Other possibilities could no doubt be envisaged.

The American response was halting and characteristically manipulative. Devices were sought to exacerbate the factionalism in the communist movement, which might have been feasible, but to do so without grasping the policy nettle. For example, since the United States had scored a propaganda success by obtaining and publishing Khrushchev's secret speech denouncing Stalin in 1956 (whether it was the complete text of the speech is still not clear), the dissemination of materials publicizing the confusion over the Sino-Soviet conflict, which did not explicitly come out into the open until 1960, appeared to be a good gambit. Apart from propaganda devices, black and white, the one serious response to the communist rift was the pronouncement that United States policy toward communism would be "differentiated," since, as Secretary of State Rusk stated, "The Communist world is no longer a simple flock of sheep following blindly behind one leader."[2] That is to say, the United States would treat with communist countries which showed their independence of Moscow. The policy was not new; Tito's Yugoslavia was one precedent, Gomulka's Poland was another, but now, significantly, post-revolt Hungary and even Rumania came within the new dispensation. The policy of differentiated treatment toward communist countries conformed to the contours of President Kennedy's American University address (see pp. 152-53), aimed at liquidating the cold war. It appeared as if American policy-makers had finally come to terms with the significance of the Sino-Soviet rift—that is, Khrushchev's attempt to improve relations with the United States even at the expense of support of his most powerful communist ally, China. But the countercurrents in American policy, rooted in ideological anticommunism, continued to frustrate the direction of policy which Kennedy apparently tried to chart.

UNITED STATES COUNTERINSURGENCY

Khrushchev's policy of peaceful coexistence and his rift with Mao Tse-tung contributed to one important development in American policy presumably not anticipated by the Soviet leader. Whatever the aims of his policy, he certainly did not envisage the possibility that American policy would become more belligerent as a consequence of his effort to allay apprehensions of Soviet-American hostilities. But this was precisely what developed, a "logical" attempt to exploit the weakness inherent in the communist rift. Since peaceful coexistence implied at the very least the avoidance of general war, the doctrine was concocted in Washington that the Soviet leaders, eschewing big wars to further revolution (to "export" it), would now pursue their revolutionary aims through internal (civil, guerrilla) warfare. The formal justification of this policy was derived from a literal reading of Soviet support for "national liberation movements" and "wars of national liberation." At the risk of some repetition of Part I, it might be useful to recapitulate communist doctrine on national liberation.

From its earliest history, communist strategy in the colonial and semicolonial areas—roughly equivalent to what we now designate as the "underdeveloped countries"—had been designed to support movements seeking freedom from foreign rule or directed against non-communist regimes with which Soviet Russia was at odds. In so doing the Soviet strategists were confronted with a basic dilemma which has remained unsolved. Since most of the liberation movements were non-communist in composition, such as the Indian Congress, and communist movements were by comparison small if they existed at all, the choice had to be made whether to support the "bourgeois" nationalist movement or the indigenous communist movement. To support the bourgeois nationalists meant that the indigenous communist movement would have to subordinate its own objectives to aid the more limited objectives of the former. If instead the Communists elected to pursue their own revolutionary aims, their prospects of success, given their weakness, would be generally nil, and they would further risk alienating those who were backing the major non-communist forces, if not exposing themselves outright to repression. The question of whom to support was usually decided in terms of Soviet state interests. Precedent was established as early as the Second Comintern Congress in 1920 where Lenin argued against the purist revolutionary ideas of M. N. Roy in favor of supporting national movements whose efforts might weaken the control of the metropolitan powers in areas adjacent to Soviet Russia, and environs—for example, British rule in Persia or foreign influence in China. Lenin's policy here, as mostly elsewhere, was a realistic one based on the existing power distribution. The interest of communist revolution was rationalized by the introduction of the idea of "stages,"—that is, the bourgeois nationalist movement was considered to be a preliminary and hence necessary stage to set the conditions for the communist seizure of power. By definition, then, the bourgeois movement became "revolutionary," justifying communist support of and subordination to it. That there was no necessary connection between the bourgeois and communist revolutionary stages became clear over the course of time. No communist movement in the underdeveloped areas came to power through this sequence. Where they did come to power, in China and Vietnam, it was through the Maoist strategy of a communist-*led*, broadly based nationalist movement which was, after the seizure of power, structured along communist lines, skipping over the bourgeois stage in any sense of the term in traditional Marxian thought. Castro's Cuba seemingly fits this sequence but in actuality does not at all. Castro's movement against Batista could be said to have been a bourgeois movement, but it did not enjoy the support of the Communists. After the seizure of power,

Castro linked up with the Soviet Union to obtain the support necessary to preserve his independence of the United States and complementarily took in the local Communists to help him organize the country.

The Comintern experience in China in the twenties is an excellent illustration of the dilemmas of communist strategy in the underdeveloped areas. Having trained, aided, and subordinated themselves to the Kuomintang in its effort to drive foreign influence out of China and unify the country, the Communists were betrayed by Chiang Kai-shek, once they had served his purposes. Then, when they struck out on their own, they were cut to pieces in Canton. Whether the Communists would have succeeded if they had from the first pursued a purist revolutionary strategy, rejecting cooperation with the Kuomintang, is a moot question. Stalin implied that they had no choice but to cooperate with the non-communist forces, since the Kuomintang was the influential Chinese party and Chiang Kai-shek was the only national leader. The argument aside, what is pertinent is that the decision to support the national liberation movements and the form of the support has always been a function of Soviet policy. With the Chinese Communists now in the picture as a state power purveying their own line with regard to the revolutionary movements, the basic dilemma —state versus indigenous communist—has not fundamentally changed. For the Chinese as for the Soviet Communists, the decision to support a revolutionary movement depends primarily on their respective relations with the government within whose territory the movement operates. Since colonial rule has virtually ended, the question is no longer one of support of revolutionary movements against foreign occupying powers. If, for example, the Chinese Communists have a prime interest in promoting African-Asian solidarity, they cannot simultaneously attempt to associate themselves closely with the Egyptian government and to promote revolution to overthrow it—or not very profitably. Similarly with the Soviet Communists. Support of national liberation movements, then, is an article of faith for all Communists but more importantly a matter of practical politics which requires choices all along the line concerning the execution or nonexecution of the strategy. The choices of strategy have also been complicated by the Sino-Soviet dispute, which has become intensely involved with national liberation movements.

Both the Chinese and the Soviet Communists support national revolutionary movements, but they invest them with different priorities and significance. To the Chinese, the "contradiction between the oppressed nations of Asia, Africa, and Latin America, and the imperialists headed by the United States is the most prominent and most acute of all the basic contradictions and is the principal contradiction in the contemporary world."[3] The United States is singled out as the chief enemy, the principal target of attack, and the revolutionary movements are designated as the chief area in which the imperialist system can be destroyed. Orthodoxy, the true measure of a "Marxist-Leninist," is determined by the acceptance of these propositions. In the Chinese book, consequently, the Soviet Communists are not "Marxist-Leninists" but "revisionists" for downgrading revolutionary strategy in the underdeveloped areas. In the Soviet scheme, the central point is "peaceful coexistence," which implies accommodation with, not unremitting hostility against, the United States. Within this framework, revolutionary agitation in the underdeveloped areas is relegated to a secondary position—it is not the central contradiction. The Russians here, let it be said, are not writing off communism's prospects in the countries of Asia, Africa, and Latin America, and they do support various governments and movements politically, economically, and militarily. What they are arguing, however, is that the movement of the underdeveloped countries toward communism can best be advanced in an atmosphere of Soviet-American *détente*, free from the threat of general war or warlike or tense situations that can develop into war. In the framework of peaceful coexistence, the Soviet theoreticians argue, the underdeveloped countries can most advantageously develop their institutions, bypassing, with communist assistance, the capitalist stage of development.

The strategies in the underdeveloped areas serve Chinese and Soviet state interests respectively. To what extent these strategies are manipulative rather than operational is difficult to say. Both Soviet and Chinese Communists may be less interested in promoting revolution in the underdeveloped areas than would be apparent from their formal positions. Yet one thing is clear: Soviet strategy toward the underdeveloped areas is a function of peaceful coexistence, and—to return to American counterinsurgency doctrine—the fomenting of internal war as a substitute for creating the conditions for revolution through general war is not part of Soviet policy. On this point, as on many others, the Chinese charges against Khrushchev and his successors are accurate.

The United States doctrine of counterinsurgency, developed under the Kennedy administration, was designed to meet presumed American interests in the underdeveloped areas, initially in Vietnam. It was rooted not in actual Soviet policy or in even a reasonable reading of the then current Soviet doctrine on the underdeveloped areas but in a myth that was easy to "sell" in Washington and to the American people because of the deeply ingrained ideology with regard to the Soviet Union and communism. Counterinsurgency met the needs of American expansionist aims, seen in terms of the proclivity of American policy to influence the direction of the underdeveloped areas— by force, if necessary. The doctrine was then generalized for all the underdeveloped areas, including Latin America, where the focus of attention became the existence of insurgent forces and the means of countering them. Recognizing that counterforce is insufficient to insure stability in these areas, the concept of "modernization" was "married" to the doctrine of counterinsurgency. Policy would be implemented on two simultaneous fronts, so to speak—military and economic, including the building of political institutions. On paper, the prospectus did not look bad. In practice, it did not work out so well, *vide* Vietnam. Its implications were fraught with danger because they involved the exercise of American force to eliminate or contain communism everywhere, and the ability of the Americans to manipulate socioeconomic and political patterns to produce stability and loyalty among the population. Realism has become equated with the exercise of force, rather than with the strategic interests of American requirements and political possibility.

Khrushchev's reorientation of Soviet policy toward an accommodation with the United States and a relaxation of world tensions was met then paradoxically with the development of a more aggressive American policy. Not that there was a neat cause-and-effect relationship; American policy also showed some tendencies toward accommodation, of which more will be said in the next chapter. Rather, cautious Soviet policy, the presumed responsibility of the United States to contain communism in Southeast Asia, and the Sino-Soviet rift combined to influence the direction of American policy. Instead of capitalizing on the Sino-Soviet rift to press for closer understanding with the Soviet Union, the United States chose to exploit the rift by pursuing a more aggressive policy in Vietnam on the assumption that the Chinese and the Russians would not coordinate and give all-out support to the Vietnamese. This calculation proved to be accurate, since the Russians did not wish to become embroiled in a war in an area outside their strategic interests—note that support of national revolutionary struggles, even those led by Communists, takes a back seat in Soviet policy. Yet the consequences of American policy tend to drive the Communists closer together, to provide the cogent argument for the re-establishment of communist international unity, and to drive the Vietnamese Communists into the arms of the Chinese Communists. The Russians were placed in a most unenviable position, caught as they were between their desire to see an end to the war and their wish to support their com-

munist comrades, between their concern to maintain
their leadership in the international communist movement and their unwillingness to risk state interests by
supporting communist Vietnam to the hilt. Obviously
the Sino-Soviet rift played into American hands. Yet
American policy in Vietnam was pursued at some cost
to Soviet-American relations and at some risk that
communist internationalism would be restored. Quite
apart from the justification of American policy, the
Vietnam case serves to illustrate the conditioning effect
of American courses of action on trends in the communist movement and on the development of polycentrism.

8. THE SOVIET-AMERICAN DÉTENTE

A curious paradox of Soviet-American relations has been the compatibility of their strategic interests despite the incompatibility of their socioeconomic systems.[1] For example, one of the factors figuring in the American recognition of the Soviet Union in 1933 was the common interest in protecting China against Japanese incursions. With the rise of fascism in Europe in the 1930s, American interests lay with the Soviet attempt to forge a viable system of collective security against the obvious revisionist tendencies of Nazi Germany. Active involvement of the United States at that time might well have blunted Nazi expansionism and the outbreak of war. Again, Franklin D. Roosevelt's prospectus for a new world order and an effective international security organization was candidly posited on a concert of the Great Powers, primarily on Soviet-American cooperation. Despite the disillusionment with Soviet policy that set in after the conclusion of hostilities and the ridicule of American postwar planning and objectives squarely based on Soviet-American cooperation, it appears more and more that Roosevelt was the realist and that the so-called realists, the latter-day "hard-liners" against the Soviet Union, have led American policy into a dead end. Once again in the 1960s, the Soviet Union appears as America's natural ally in Asia, this time as a bulwark against Chinese expansionism there. The key country in Asia is India, not Vietnam or Laos, and here the United States and the USSR join interests in securing India's sovereignty. Soviet refusal to back the Chinese in their border dispute with India was one of the signal political developments of the times and clearly in American foreign-policy interest. Americans have only to speculate on the possibilities of tension and actual conflict that might have occurred had the Soviet Union unequivocally backed its erstwhile communist ally against India. In Europe too, though it may be less obvious, stability is dependent on Soviet-American agreement, primarily as it involves the future of the still-unsettled German problem. As matters stand, the United States is a hostage to the Berlin enclave in East Germany, subject to the manipulation of tension there as suits Soviet interests. The fate of Germany is, in the last analysis, in the hands of the Russians, who have East Germany to deal out as their trump card if the question of German reunification becomes serious. A new Rapallo may not be the predictable line of development, but a realignment removing West Germany as the linchpin of American policy in Europe as a result of Soviet concessions on reunification may well be. Or, in the remote possibility of an indigenous all-German reunification drive, United States interests would again dovetail with Soviet in maintaining stability on the continent.

Less tangible but of overwhelming concern is the compatibility of Soviet-American interest in avoiding war and investing substance into the slogan of peaceful coexistence. So accustomed has the world become to war and destruction that it has become banal to mention the simple fact that the United States and the USSR have the capability of destroying each other as well as any other parts of the world that get in their way. This is the reality—not the sick reality of the Chinese Communists who purport to envision the construction of a socialist society on the ruins of nuclear devastation, or that of the American politico-military theorists who are "courageous" enough to think about the unthinkable. These latter merely express the neuroses of a world that approaches political bankruptcy and are acting out the "death instinct." It is to the credit of Khrushchev that, coming to terms with the nuclear reality, he proposed to liquidate the cold war. In his attempt to do so, he precipitated the deepest and probably most lasting schism in the history of the international communist movement, sacrificing the Chinese alliance to efforts at accommodation with the United States. The behavior of his successors confirms Khrushchev's policy not as a personal aberration but as the central policy of the Soviet government.

In contrast, American response to Soviet overtures for the liquidation of the cold war has been slow in coming, tentative, and ambiguous. There are many reasons why this has been so. The United States is the stronger of the two powers and feels less need to rush into any accommodation. The United States policy of world-wide alliances and the aggressive outward thrust of its influence is predicated, to a large extent, on opposition to the Soviet Union. *Détente* with the Soviet Union would throw into question the very basis of American policy, although there has already been an erosion of policy and institutions in response to the *de facto* shift in Soviet policy, the Atlantic alliance, for example. Distrust and suspicion of the Soviet Union will, however, wither slowly, if at all. Rightly or wrongly, alleged Soviet responsibility for the cold war, the satellization of East-Central Europe, the aggressive strategy of the late 1940s, the Korean war, the suppression of the Hungarian revolt and other events have contributed to create an attitude to the Soviet Union which, reinforced by internal propaganda, is almost impregnably hostile. American society has been progressively centralized, bureaucratized, and militarized as its material welfare has expanded, making it easier to manipulate policy and absorb dissent. Young Americans, brought up in an atmosphere of violence and war, expect no more. The older generation, once burned by association with, or miscalculation of, communism and Soviet policy, is neutralized when it does not actively support the policies of the Establishment.

Apart from the flash of the Camp David spirit, which was widely regarded in Washington as "dangerous," and the aborted summit meeting in 1960 in Geneva, which conversely was greeted widely in Washington with relief, since it "demonstrated" that Khrushchev really did not desire to reduce tensions, the one top-level attempt to readjust American policy occurred in the third year of the Kennedy administration. In what may turn out to be one of his most significant speeches, President Kennedy called for a re-examination of the

American attitude toward the cold war: "Let us re-examine our attitude toward the cold war. . . . We must deal with the world as it is and not as it might have been had the history of the last eighteen years been different."[2]

Continuity in this trend of thought after Johnson's succession to the presidency was maintained in Secretary Rusk's public defense of the Administration's differentiated approach to various communist countries. The Secretary informed an audience of laymen that the Soviet Union was beginning to behave more nearly like a normal state: "They [the rulers of the Soviet Union] appear to have begun to realize that there is an irresolvable contradiction between the demands to promote world Communism by force and the needs of and interests of the Soviet state and people."[3] Adlai E. Stevenson, then United States representative at the United Nations, used the 1964 Dag Hammarskjöld Memorial Lecture to suggest that "we have begun to move beyond the policy of containment" to a "policy of cease-fire, and peaceful change."[4] In other words, picking its way cautiously through the highly emotional and politically charged landscape of anticommunism in this country, the Administration appeared to be rationalizing its position in a more systematic way before the American public.

One concrete result of Kennedy's cautious attempt to improve Soviet-American relations (the installation of direct communication between Moscow and Washington was also noteworthy) was the test-ban treaty of July 1963, which was designed to reduce the risk of war and indicated a common Soviet-American interest in preventing the proliferation of nuclear weapons, as well as in putting a stop to the contamination of the atmosphere. Both signatories had to suffer partners—France and Communist China—who refused to adhere to the treaty. Since it is always the Soviet Union's good faith that is at issue, it should be noted that China accompanied its refusal to sign with violent denunciations of the USSR for having sold out to American "imperialism," and the attitude of the various communist parties toward the treaty became one more criterion governing pro-Moscow or pro-Peking orientation. Though by 1963 the treaty cannot be said to have been the straw that broke the dragon's back, nevertheless its conclusion may have been particularly aggravating to the Chinese, who disclosed that the Russians had reneged in 1959 on their promise to help develop China's atomic capability.[5] The negotiation of the treaty was important not only in itself but as part of the creation of an environment in which such minor aspects of Soviet-American relations as exchange of persons could be handled in a freer manner, and in which such major problems as reduction of armaments could be negotiated.

Whether Soviet-American relations would have continued a steady improvement had Kennedy lived and been re-elected cannot, of course, be stated with any certainty. Despite its intellectual courtiers, the Kennedy administration had shown no particular flair for international affairs. It was responsible for one of the biggest fiascos in recent times, the Bay of Pigs, and the "victory" over Khrushchev in the Cuban missile crisis was the product of a situation created by the ineptness of the Administration. Similarly, the Alliance for Progress, or what might be called an attempt at controlled middle-class revolution-from-above, was an unfruitful policy in Latin America as was the Administration's policy for and against Diem in Vietnam. For Kennedy as for his successor, domestic politics were the greater reality, making it expedient to move with extreme caution in the direction of improvement of relations with communist countries while action against communism, however justified, reaped domestic support (even in the face of domestic criticism on Vietnam in 1965). In Kennedy's favor, however, was his face-down of Khrushchev on Cuba and, as a result, a certain confidence—a mutual respect and understanding—that had favorable repercussions on the improvement of Soviet-American relations.

The personal contact was lost with Kennedy's assassination in 1963 and Khrushchev's ouster the next year, but the basis for Soviet-American cooperation transcended personalities. Both the Johnson administration —which retained Kennedy's chief foreign-policy advisers, McGeorge Bundy, Special Assistant to the President for National Security Affairs; Secretary of Defense Robert S. McNamara; and Secretary of State Dean Rusk—and the Brezhnev-Kosygin government reaffirmed the lines followed by their predecessors. Yet the old habits persisted. Johnson chose to force the communist-led Vietnamese out of South Vietnam by a major commitment of American military power. Quite apart from the merits of the Johnson policy in Vietnam, it could serve only to retard the betterment of Soviet-American relations. However little the Soviet leaders cared whether Vietnam were united under communist auspices in 1965—of the three big powers involved, the United States, China, and the USSR, the last appears to be the least interested in wars of national liberation —they could not simply ignore the fate of a fraternal communist state, particularly when their leadership of international communism was being challenged by the Chinese Communists. Within the United States, Johnson's incursion into Vietnam in force had the predictable effect of intensifying the anticommunist virus, with opponents or critics of policy exposed to charges of being procommunist, unpatriotic, or at best stupid. United States policy-makers could point with pride to their successful exploitation of the Sino-Soviet conflict and the rift in the international communist movement, were it not that the venture in Vietnam is, at least to this writer, strategically unsound, politically self-defeating, and morally indefensible, and in addition jeopardizes relations with the country on which, together with the United States, the peace of the world depends.

9. SUMMING UP

In historical perspective, communist internationalism represents one more failure by man to form a political association that would transcend national boundaries. There is no certainty that a world organized by an international authority, on communist or other lines, would necessarily provide the environment for man to lead a freer and better life, to ennoble himself and achieve happiness. Violence and aggression may be in the nature of man, and repression and regimentation (civilization) may be the necessary corollary of any social order, national or international. Yet man's constant attempt to escape the limitations of the present has impelled him to search for alternative forms of political and socioeconomic organization and for internationalist solutions, if for no other reason than the seemingly restrictive, irrational, and murderous implications of a world ordered on nationalist lines. Marxism, a product of the eighteenth- and nineteenth-century belief in human progress and perfectibility, expressed man's longing for a rational order in the late nineteenth and early twentieth centuries. Nineteenth-century capitalism, dehumanizing the workers through its crudely exploitative system, was viewed through the prism of its possibilities—that is, a developing international economic system potentially capable of providing abundance to the workers of the world through a rational organization that would transcend the national boundaries being rendered obsolete by technologically advanced methods of production and distribution. Freed of the need to engage in exhaustive labor and of the threat of war implicit in national rivalry, man could leap from the realm of necessity to the realm of freedom. He would be free to develop his potentialities to the fullest; who could imagine what flowering of human nature would spring from the release of man's inner resources?

The socialist and communist internationals were the organizational manifestations of this vision. The vision died hard. The first failure lay in the assertion of patriotism of the members of the Second (Socialist) International who opted to defend their respective governments with which the workers' interests were by then identified. To Lenin this represented a failure of will against which he attempted to insure in the future by developing a highly centralized international organization. This, the Third (Communist) International, also failed, quickly and abysmally, in the first years of the 1920s. The artificial attempt to maintain the Marxian vision of world revolution through the agency of the Soviet Union, which held all these hopes as it were in trusteeship, also collapsed, as the centrifugal tendencies in the communist movement developed, first with Yugoslavia's assertion of independence and then with the fragmentation of the movement in the post-Stalinist era.

The collapse of international communist unity underscores the priority of national particularism in its hold on man's loyalties. Nationalism represents the higher reality. It is not necessarily rational or welcome or to be accepted for all time, but it is the unavoidable fact of international politics. Yet the internationalism of the communist movement, in either its unified or its fragmented form, while not irrelevant to American interests, was and is decidedly of minor relevance compared to the power potential and direction of interests of the various communist nation-states. To put it another way, American obsession with "international communism" has frustrated the development of a realistic policy toward the communist states and, in more recent times, toward radical nationalist movements which are, by the obsessional identification of radicalism with communism, suspect.

Evil is dialectically intertwined with good. The Soviet Union and international communism have served as the incarnation of evil for Americans,[1] contributing to what Erich Fromm has called pathological thinking about Russia. In the familiar psychological mechanism of "projection": "The enemy appears as the embodiment of all evil because all evil that I feel in myself is projected on to him. Logically, after this has happened, I consider myself as the embodiment of all good since the evil has been transferred to the other side. The result is indignation and hatred against the enemy and uncritical, narcissistic self-glorification."[2] Thus the nature of "good" has been defined as the defense of the "free world," a term devoid of all political, social, and moral content, meaning simply the non-communist or anticommunist world. Some are more sophisticated, knowing that the "free world" is less than free and that the communist world is less than evil. Some, self-styled realists, pretend to ignore all moral factors, basing policy on the criterion of "national interest." Yet the framework of the dialectical antipodes remains, a convenient cover to pursue one policy or another with the backing of anticommunism. Thus, the fission of the international communist movement has altered policy and attitude very slightly: there are now two brands of international communism, with the Chinese perhaps more revolting than the Soviet.

Similarly, the post-Stalin developments in the USSR have been "welcomed": the curbing of the secret police, the emphasis on improving the standard of living, the experimentation with nondirective economic policies, and, in the realm of foreign policy, an attempt to liquidate the cold war and improve Soviet-American relations. But the United States has conceded very little to put Soviet-American relations on a new basis. To liquidate the cold war requires compromise and a rearrangement of priorities, which implies the sacrifice of certain positions. Quite apart from what bargains the Soviet leaders would be willing to strike, the United States is ill disposed to yield at all in Europe, to relinquish any commitments in Asia and elsewhere, and to take risks that might improve Soviet-American relations. Thus, in spite of the significant changes in Soviet policy, it remains the "enemy," not merely the chief "opponent," "adversary," or great power "rival." The distinction between "enemy" and "opponent" is

not an unimportant one.[3] One traffics with the enemy
—in the hope of his eventual annihilation. One opposes
and competes with an opponent, without, however,
regarding the struggle as one of life or death. No law
of history determines that the stakes are survival or
destruction. Clarification of this difference might be
useful in molding American attitudes toward the Soviet Union. Even in connection with their brief forays
toward improving Soviet-American relations, United
States policy-makers have, however, failed to make a
concerted effort to clear the atmosphere in this country, at least to the point of reducing the popular obsession with communism in favor of a more realistic view.
Perhaps it is too much to expect politically sensitive
policy-makers to undertake the most unpopular task
of minimizing anticommunism. Yet it is the responsibility of policy-makers to clarify, not confuse, issues
—and understanding begins at home.[4] If the policy-
makers are captives of ideological anticommunism to
which they contribute actively and by omission in their
daily utterances, they are doubly inhibited in essaying
any policy initiatives.

Although there has been an abundance of comment
on the split in the international communist movement,
there has not been much written on its policy implications. It is undoubtedly the better part of wisdom to
avoid speculation on the precise policy directions this
profound development might take. Yet already certain
seemingly strange features have taken shape which are
worth notice. The Chinese Communists, freed of the
restraints imposed upon them by Khrushchev's peaceful coexistence policy, have nevertheless pursued a
remarkably cautious foreign policy. This would seem

a valid over-all appraisal, even in the light of their actions in India and Southeast Asia. The boldness of their action has been in inverse relation to their invective. The split with the Soviet Union has removed the shackles on the free expression of their views and on their diplomacy in the underdeveloped areas, some of which is a product of the split, an attempt to increase their influence vis-à-vis the Soviet Union, but the pursuit of policy has been limited by their economic and political weakness. This is evident in their frustration with regard to Formosa and most revealingly, at the time this is written, with regard to the Vietnam war. The split with the Soviet Union has removed their protective military umbrella, and political maneuver as well as direct action is inhibited.

For the Soviet Union, the split with the Chinese has been doubly inhibitory. On the one side, its attempted *détente* with the United States has yielded very little tangible return, either in terms of a European settlement, which still appears to hold first priority, or in the reduction of armaments which would release resources for internal development. On the other side, the split with the Chinese has weakened its authority in the international communist movement and its hold over such communist states as North Korea and North Vietnam or such important non-ruling communist parties as the Indonesian, whose policy interests seemed to coincide more nearly with the Chinese. The less the payoff from its coexistence policy, the greater the pressure on it from its "hards" both inside the Soviet Union and the Communists-at-large. Whereas formerly its sacrifice of communist interests to its own state interests did not weaken Soviet authority in the international communist movement—though the results might have weakened a particular communist party— it now defaults to Chinese leadership and to the self-assertion of the individual communist parties.

The United States has profited automatically from the split in the international communist movement and the falling out of the two major communist powers. It has taken advantage of the split in one major policy action—Vietnam, where it has chosen to escalate the war, on the calculation, among others, that the split would prevent concerted counter-action. United States action was taken on the chance that it might impair Soviet-American relations temporarily but not over a longer span. The calculation may have been warranted, but the prior question is whether the Vietnam action was itself warranted—if only in view of its possible harmful effect on Soviet-American relations. The problem is one of priority of policy and feasibility of strategy. In the writer's view, the prospects of a successful American operation in Vietnam were never propitious. A political community cannot be called into being by fiat, even if the fiat is handed down by the United States.

The long and short of it is that American policy in Vietnam during the past decade was designed to frustrate the Geneva Convention, which, through the face-saving device of elections, would have conceded all Vietnam to the victorious communist-led Vietminh. Two separate states were not contemplated. Nevertheless, American policy was directed toward the creation of an independent South Vietnamese state as a buffer against communism. Yet the ever-increasing commitment of military, economic, and technical resources failed to establish a viable South Vietnamese political authority, and, when it appeared that the country would fall to the communist-led rebels, President Johnson opted to commit American troops in force. The unstated objective of American policy is now to maintain an American presence in Southeast Asia to act as a deterrent to the Chinese.

Once again all the clichés of American policy were invoked. The United States was containing international communism in Southeast Asia, though the nature of this international communism was obscure—the directing center of international communism, in fact, nonexistent. The USSR had little influence on the policy of the Democratic Republic of Vietnam and was clearly unhappy about the escalation of the war. The Chinese, into whose hands American policy played, had little demonstrably to do with the war. American action, moreover, tended to force the DRV to look to the communist countries for assistance and, in the last analysis, to depend on Communist China for its defense. Put another way, the effect of American action was to give sustenance to any forces at work to reconstruct the unity of the communist movement—to bring back into being what it said it was fighting against. Of course, American opinion-makers could have simply stated that the United States was fighting to maintain its position in Southeast Asia, which would not have altered the strategic picture or the advisability of the action but would at least have helped wipe out one of the fictions of American policy. But "international communism" serves the policy-makers well as an incantation to incite the American people.

The open American resort to war in Vietnam represented a failure of American policy which the Johnson administration refused to acknowledge. It lacked the courage either to concede failure, as the French did in Vietnam and Algeria, and negotiate a way out that involved loss of position and influence, or to install an open military occupation. These were distasteful options for a country which engages in the substance of imperialism but balks at the form. Indeed, United States policy in Vietnam illustrates the vulnerabilities and shortcomings for which American policy has so often been criticized: the assertion of omnipotence which impels the United States to become involved in global political problems without proper discrimination; the failure to define strategic requirements and priorities; the penchant for moralizing and sanctifying its policies while manipulating political and legal agreements to suit its purposes and engaging in reprehensible and cruel action; the failure to take into account historical and political realities; and the pseudo-realism, in reaction to Wilsonian and Rooseveltian "idealism," which tends to equate realism with the absence of principle and morality and with the exercise of force.

But this book is not intended to range over the whole spectrum of American policy, nor is it intended to prescribe a policy that would fit a particular *Weltanschauung*. Yet, given the conservative bent of the United States—indeed, precisely because of it—the developments over the past decade in the Soviet Union and in international communism hold out a policy alternative that is objectively in the interest of American security and world peace. It is, moreover, an alternative that has been recognized by the policy-makers and to some extent acted upon—namely, to scuttle the policy of undiscriminating anticommunism in favor of establishing a *modus vivendi* with the Soviet Union. As an Asian power, the United States has two potential allies, Japan on the east shore of the Pacific, which prefers to remain tranquilized, and the Soviet Union on the west. In Europe, still the most important political area of the world and the one area with which the United States has rapport, peace and progress depend on an understanding with the Soviet Union. A rapprochement with the Soviet Union contributes to, as tension would detract from, the vaunted American purpose of "freeing" the Central-Eastern European states. Although Eastern Europe is, and for some time at least will remain, in the Soviet security sphere, these countries are moving toward the independent exercise of power and the amelioration of the conditions of their citizens. A Soviet-American rapprochement is no panacea for the ills of this world of nation-states, which are probably incurable. It makes sense, nevertheless, for the two great powers to reach understandings which might mitigate the possibilities of war. The creation of a general framework of understanding would also help establish ground rules for the inevitable Soviet-American competition in the underdeveloped areas. De-emphasis on the struggle against international communism, accompanied by a measure of de-indoctrination within the United States, which is a logical concomitant of policy, would be a healthy internal development. These and others are reasons for taking advantage of the legacy bequeathed by Khrushchev to his successors, who have given every indication of continuing his policies of accommodation with the West and rejection of the Chinese Communist positions of unrelenting hostility toward the United States and incitement of international conflict. Whether the Russians continue to hold their present views depends to a large, if indeterminate, extent on what the United States does. It is time to drop the old cliché that the United States only reacts to Soviet policy. Quite the contrary. What the Soviet Union does and the direction international communism takes depend in large measure on the policy and attitude of the United States.

NOTES

Chapter 1

1. Borkenau, Franz. *World Communism.* New York: Norton, 1939, pp. 366 ff.

2. See Benjamin Schwartz's perceptive article, "Sino-Soviet Relations—The Question of Authority," in Zagoria, Donald S., ed., "Communist China and the Soviet Bloc," *The Annals of the American Academy of Political and Social Science,* Vol. 349 (September 1963), pp. 38-48.

3. Although contemporary organization theorists have not concerned themselves particularly with communism, there is much suggestive comment in their writing. Thus, Gross summarized Herbert Simon: "Authority cannot be fully understood as a legal phenomenon or as based on formal sanctions alone. A person will accept orders not merely because of the fear of punishment but also because of willingness to achieve the organization's purpose, a disinclination to accept responsibility, a psychological willingness or desire to follow a leader or the social sanctions imposed by the group to which he belongs." (Gross, Bertram M. *The Managing of Organizations: The Administrative Struggle.* New York: The Free Press, 1964, Vol. I, p. 186.)

4. Thus, in a retrospect by a French Communist: "The attachment of the Communists throughout the world to Stalin was not so much to Stalin as a man, *but to Stalin as the symbol of the cause and reality of socialism.*" (Verret, Michel, in *La Nouvelle Critique,* Paris, December 1963, p. 44.)

5. "Manifesto of the Communist International to the Proletariat of the Entire World," March 6, 1919, in Degras, Jane, ed., *The Communist International, 1919-1943*. London: Oxford University Press, 1956, Vol. I (1919-1922), pp. 38-47.

6. *The Foundation of the Communist International*. New York: International Publishers, 1934, p. 3.

7. Roy, M. N. *The Communist International*. Delhi: Radical Democratic Party, 1943.

8. Prefacing his discussion of the relationship of the intellectuals to the French Communist Party, David Caute has emphasized the point that their support and even obedience were offered within the context of free adherence and the right of free withdrawal, but the dilemma of freedom and necessity, seen both in philosophical and psychological terms, is far from simple and never easily resolved. (*Communism and the French Intellectuals, 1914-1960*. London: André Deutsch, 1964, pp. 12, 16.) While the point—which applies in countries not controlled by the Communists to intellectuals and nonintellectuals alike—may seem obvious, it has been lost sight of under the blanket of theories stressing allegiance through physical fear, personal aberrations, and the like.

9. Laski, Harold J. *A Grammar of Politics*. London: G. Allen and Unwin, 1925, p. 258.

10. Kennan, George F. "Soviet-American Relations, 1917-1920," *The Decision to Intervene*, Vol. II. Princeton: Princeton University Press, 1958, p. 404. Also Williams, William A. "American Intervention in Russia, 1917-1920," *Studies on the Left*, Vol. III, No. 4 (1963), p. 42.

11. "Thus the weak power position of the early Soviet Republic and the Marxist myth of proletarian internationalism, reinforcing each other, led to emphasis on world revolution and World Communism as Soviet policy goals," according to John H. Kautsky. ("Myth, Self-fulfilling Prophecy, and Symbolic Reassurance in the East-West Conflict," *The Journal of Conflict Resolution*, Vol. IX, No. 1 [March 1965], pp. 1-17.) Kautsky has some stimulating comments on the role of myth in Soviet-American antagonism.

12. Borkenau, Franz. *Socialism: National and International*. London: George Routledge and Sons, 1942, *passim*.

Chapter 2

1. The Cominform (Information Bureau of the Communist and Workers' Parties, 1947-1956) was a regional and limited organization which differed from the Comintern in purpose, membership, and function (see page 41).

2. Duverger, Maurice. *Political Parties*, 2d ed. New York: Wiley, 1963, pp. 150-51.

3. Balabanoff, Angelica. *My Life as a Rebel*. New York: Harper, 1938, p. 209.

4. Lenin, V. I. *Collected Works*. New York: International Publishers, 1930, Vol. XVIII, pp. 82 and 59-213 *passim*.

5. Eberlein, Hugo (Max Albert). "Osnovanie Kominterna i Spartakovskii Sojus," *Kommunisticheskii Internatsional*, Nos. 187-188 (1929), p. 194.

6. Hulse, James W. *The Forming of the Communist International*. Stanford, Calif.: Stanford University Press, 1964, pp. 192-93.

7. Trotsky, Leon. "On the Coming Congress of the Comintern," *The First Five Years of the Communist International*. New York: Pioneer Publishers, 1945, Vol. I, chap. 10, pp. 84-85.

8. *Ibid.*, p. 84.

9. Trotsky. "En Route: Thoughts on the Progress of the Proletarian Revolution." *Op. cit.*, Vol. I, pp. 62-63.

10. Friedrich, Carl J. *Man and His Government*. New York: McGraw-Hill, 1963, p. 397.

11. "The fact of the matter is that the socialist and radical movements in this country, as in all other countries outside Russia, came to a dead end in 1914. When the largest and strongest socialist parties of Europe, along with the movements of the anarchists and syndicalists, collapsed under the test of the First World War, a question mark was put over the perspectives of socialism everywhere. Socialists everywhere groped in darkness, questioning their previous assumptions.

"Light came finally from the East. The Bolshevik party of Russia was the one party that demonstrated in action its capacity to cope with the problems of war and revolution. For that reason it became the inspiring center for a revival and regroupment of the revolutionary workers in all countries of the globe, including the United States whose previous movement had been the most primitive, isolationist, and politically backward of them all." (Cannon, James P. *The First Ten Years of American Communism: Report of a Participant*. New York: Lyle Stuart, 1962, pp. 322-23.)

12. Weldon, Thomas D. *The Vocabulary of Politics*. London: Penguin, 1953, p. 54.

13. See, for example, McKenzie, Kermit E. *Comintern and World Revolution, 1928-1943*. New York: Columbia University Press, 1964, pp. 295-96.

14. Max Schachtman in Trotsky, Leon, *The Third International After Lenin*, John G. Wright, trans. New York: Pioneer Publishers, 1957, p. 358.

15. *The Communist International, op. cit.*, pp. 4-5.

16. *Kommunisticheskii Internatsional*, No. 5-6, pp. 8-10.

17. Lenin, V. I. "Preliminary Draft of Theses on the National and Colonial Questions," *Selected Works*. Moscow: Foreign Languages Publishing House, 1947, Vol. II, p. 657.

18. Kautsky, John H. *Moscow and the Communist Party of India.* Cambridge, Mass.: Technical Press of Massachusetts Institute of Technology, 1956.

19. Under this definition, the international communist movement has been polycentric since Tito's assertion of independence in 1948. At that time, however, Yugoslavia was considered to be outside the movement, thus preserving by definition, if not in fact, the movement's monocentrist character.

20. Palmiro Togliatti's concept of a "polycentric system" was one in which there was "full autonomy of the individual Communist parties and of bilateral relations between them to establish complete, mutual understanding and complete, mutual trust, conditions necessary for collaboration and to give unity to the Communist movement itself and to the entire progressive movement of the working class." ("Report to the Central Committee of the Italian Communist Party," June 24, 1956, in Columbia University, Russian Institute, *The Anti-Stalin Campaign and International Communism.* New York: Columbia University Press, 1956, pp. 215-16.)

21. Bass, Robert, and Elizabeth Marbury, eds. "Joint Soviet-Yugoslav Declaration" (Belgrade, June 2, 1955), *The Soviet-Yugoslav Controversy, 1948-58: A Documentary Record.* New York: Prospect Books, 1959, pp. 55-60. The Soviet-Yugoslav position was further clarified in "Declaration on Relations Between the Yugoslav League of Communists and the Communist Party of the Soviet Union," June 20, 1956. (Paul E. Zinner, ed., *National Communism and Popular Revolt in Eastern Europe.* New York: Columbia University Press, 1956, pp. 12-15.)

22. Griffith, William E. "The November 1960 Moscow Meeting: A Preliminary Reconstruction," *The China Quarterly,* No. 11 (July–September 1962), pp. 38-57.

Chapter 3

1. Technically, two communist states in addition to the Soviet Union existed prior to World War Two: the "Tuva Peoples' Republic," incorporated into the USSR in 1944, and the "Mongolian Peoples' Republic," a virtual appendage of the USSR.

2. These assumptions did not at the time appear so farfetched to American policy-makers, who largely granted their validity in formulating policy *vis-à-vis* the communist "bloc."

3. Milovan Djilas, who was in a better position than most to know, can offer only the explanation that an open, armed clash between the USSR and Yugoslavia was averted "because it was not in Stalin's interest to risk a clash of unforeseeable proportions." (*The New Class.* New York: Praeger, 1957, p. 177.) Djilas's explanation may

be sufficient. If so, some rethinking might be in order on the nature of Soviet aggressiveness during the "forward" period.

4. "Declaration by the Government of the USSR on the Principles of Development and Further Strengthening of Friendship and Co-operation Between the Soviet Union and Other Socialist States, October 30, 1956," in Zinner, *op cit.*, p. 485.

5. "Declaration of Conference of Representatives of Communist and Workers' Parties of Socialist Countries," Moscow, November 14-17, 1957; *The Current Digest of the Soviet Press*, Vol. IX, No. 47 (January 1, 1958), pp. 3-7.

6. *L'Unità*, December 4, 1959, p. 1, carries an interview with Mario Alicata, a member of the Italian Communist Party Directorate, which throws some light on the origins and purpose of the meeting.

7. Dutt, Clemens, ed. *Fundamentals of Marxism-Leninism.* Moscow: Foreign Languages Publishing House, 1st ed., n.d., p. 375.

8. *Ibid.*, p. 406.

9. "On the Historical Experience of the Dictatorship of the Proletariat," *People's Daily*, April 5, 1956.

10. Schwartz, Harry. *Tsars, Mandarins, and Commissars.* Philadelphia: Lippincott, 1964, p. 158.

11. "The cardinal outcome of the second world war was the formation, alongside of the capitalist world camp, of a world camp of socialism and democracy, headed by the USSR, or, it would be truer to say, by the Soviet Union and the Chinese People's Republic." (Molotov's report to the Supreme Soviet on February 8, 1955. *New Times*, Supplement, February 12, 1955, No. 7, p. 11.) The special role of China in the minds of Stalin's successors may be said to have been kremlinologically revealed in Malenkov's funeral oration for Stalin when he said, "It is our sacred duty to preserve and strengthen the supreme achievement of the peoples, the camp of peace, democracy, and socialism, to strengthen the ties of friendship and solidarity of the peoples of the democratic camp. We must in every way strengthen the eternal, indestructible, fraternal friendship of the Soviet Union with the great Chinese people and with the working people of all people's democracies." (*Pravda*, March 10, 1953, p. 1.)

Chapter 4

1. Bureau of Intelligence and Research, Department of State. *World Strength of the Communist Party Organizations.* Washington, D.C., January 1965. For a detailed analysis of the communist parties in terms of size, area, population, industrial production, etc., see Triska, Jan F., with David O. Beim and Noralou Roos, *The World Communist System,* Stanford Studies of the Communist System, mimeographed.

2. *L'Unità,* September 5, 1964; English translation in *Information Bulletin,* No. 22, Toronto, Canada: Progress Books, pp. 15-26.

3. *L'Unità,* October 15, 1964, p. 12.

4. *Ibid.*

5. *Ibid.*

6. *Ibid.*

7. "The autonomy of the parties, a point we most determinedly champion, is not only the inner necessity of our movement, but also an essential requisite for our progress in the present conditions. For that reason we are against all proposals to reinstitute a centralized international organization. We are resolute partisans of unity in our movement and in the international labor movement; this unity, however, should be maintained in a situation where we have a multiplicity of concrete positions that accord with the conditions in the different countries and their levels of development." (Togliatti, Yalta Memorandum, *op. cit.*)

8. *L'Unità,* October 15, 1964, *op. cit.*

9. The formidable difficulty of reconciling internationalism with autonomy has been expressed thus by R. Palme Dutt, an old communist hand concerned with international problems and theory: "The problem of the modern phase has become to find the best means of combining the essential unity of international outlook, general strategic and tactical orientation and practical action, which is the hallmark of Marxism-Leninism and the indispensable conditions for the strength and further advance of the international communist movement, with the no less essential principle of the independence and equality of all communist parties and of all socialist states.

"This problem is not so insoluble as its abstract formulation might make it appear." Dutt places his hope in the nature of Marxism-Leninism, which is "no fixed dogma, but a living and creative theory." ... Hope springs eternal. (*The Internationale.* London: Lawrence and Wishart, 1964, pp. 319–20.)

10. *World Marxist Review,* Vol. VIII, No. 7 (July 1965), pp. 65-66; *Information Bulletin,* No. 50, Toronto, Canada: Progress Books, pp. 5-11.

Chapter 6

1. Vol. XXV, No. 4, pp. 566-82.

2. Whelan, Joseph G. "George Kennan and His Influence on American Foreign Policy," *The Virginia Quarterly Review,* Vol. XXXV (Spring 1959), pp. 201-202.

3. Kennan, George F. *Russia, the Atom, and the West.* London: Oxford University Press, 1958.

4. *Soviet Conduct in World Affairs,* edited by Alexander Dallin.

New York: Columbia University Press, 1960, contains a sampling of various approaches.

5. Address of Secretary of State Acheson before the World Organization for Brotherhood of the National Conference of Christians and Jews, Washington, D.C., November 9, 1950; Department of State, Publication 6446, *American Foreign Policy, 1950-1955*, Basic Documents. Washington, D.C.: Government Printing Office, 1957, Vol. II, pp. 13-14.

6. A description of the content of the ideology of "constitutional democracy" may be found in "Ideology and Foreign Affairs" by the Center for International Affairs, Harvard University. U.S. Senate, Committee on Foreign Relations. (*United States Foreign Policy*. Eighty-sixth Congress, second session, Washington, D.C.: Government Printing Office, Vol. II, 1960, pp. 1004-1005.)

7. Roberts, Henry L. "Russia and America" in *Russian Foreign Policy*, Ivo J. Lederer, ed. New Haven: Yale University Press, 1962, p. 591.

8. Francis, David R. *Russia from the American Embassy, April 1916–November 1918*. New York: Scribner's, 1921, p. 186.

9. Williams, William A. *The Tragedy of American Diplomacy*. New York: Delta, 1962, p. 100.

10. Kautsky, John H. *Political Change in Underdeveloped Countries: Nationalism and Communism*. New York: Wiley, 1962, p. 87.

Chapter 7

1. Bureau of Intelligence and Research, U.S. Department of State. *World Strength of the Communist Party Organizations, op. cit.,* pp. 7-14.

2. "Why We Treat Different Communists Differently," *Department of State Bulletin*, Vol. L, No. 1290 (March 16, 1964), pp. 390-96.

3. P'eng Chen, Member of the Political Bureau of the Secretariat of the Party's Central Committee, CC/CCP, Speech on May 25, 1965, at the Aliarcham Academy of Social Sciences in Jakarta. *Peking Review*, Vol. VIII, No. 24 (June 11, 1965), p. 11.

Chapter 8

1. As John Lukacs put it, "No matter how widespread their reputation as international communists promoting the cause of world-wide revolution, the rulers of Russia, including Stalin as well as Khrushchev, have consistently tried to promote a Russian-American division of

the world." (*A History of the Cold War.* New York: Anchor, 1962, p. 169.)

2. "Toward a Strategy of Peace," address delivered at the Commencement exercises of The American University, Washington, D.C., June 10, 1963, *Department of State Bulletin,* Vol. XLIX, No. 1253 (July 1, 1963), pp. 2-6.

3. Address before the annual full citizenship and world affairs conference of the International Union of Electrical, Radio and Machine Workers (AFL-CIO), Washington, February 25, 1964. "Why We Treat Different Communists Differently," *op. cit.* Compare the quoted excerpt from Rusk's speech with E. H. Carr's conclusion after the failure of the communist rising in Germany in October 1923: "Never again were the expectations of an early revolution in Germany allowed to override the normal considerations of foreign policy. Never again would Comintern pursue an independent policy of its own." (*German-Soviet Relations Between the Two World Wars, 1919-1939.* Oxford, 1952, p. 76.) Is it possible that the interpretation of the State Department is forty years behind the times?

4. *The New York Times,* March 24, 1964, p. 14.

5. Exactly what was at stake is not clear. The Chinese charged that "in June 1959, the Soviet Government unilaterally tore up the agreement on new technology for national defense concluded between China and the Soviet Union in October 1957, and refused to provide China with a sample of an atomic bomb and technical data concerning its manufacture." ("The Origin and Development of the Differences Between the Leadership of the CPSU and Ourselves," *People's Daily–Red Flag,* September 6, 1963.)

Chapter 9

1. Secretary of State Acheson, for example, once generously conceded that the two systems, ours and theirs, "good and evil," could coexist—depending largely on them. (Address delivered at the University of California, Berkeley, March 16, 1950, published in Department of State, Publication 6446, *American Foreign Policy, 1950-1955.* Washington, D.C.: Government Printing Office, 1957, p. 1930.)

2. Fromm, Erich. *May Man Prevail?* Garden City, New York: Doubleday, 1961, p. 22.

3. George F. Kennan, urging the perception of, and response to, change in Soviet policy as it occurs, has remarked that "we do suffer, after all, from a dangerous tendency to mistake any opponent of the present for our own image of the enemy of the past, to fight the specter we ourselves have created rather than the living adversary

that stands before us, and thus to mold the future in the shape of our fears rather than our hopes." "Contemporary Perspectives," in Lederer, ed., *Russian Foreign Policy, op. cit.,* p. 600.

4. Instead, in 1965 Secretary of State Rusk was still talking about "world revolution" and charging the "leaders of the other side" with responsibility for the upheavals in Vietnam, the Dominican Republic, and the Congo, as if there were some central conspiracy plotting these events and as if the Sino-Soviet split had never occurred. (Henry F. Graff, "Decision in Viet Nam, How Johnson Makes Foreign Policy," *The New York Times Magazine,* July 4, 1965, p. 16.)

INDEX